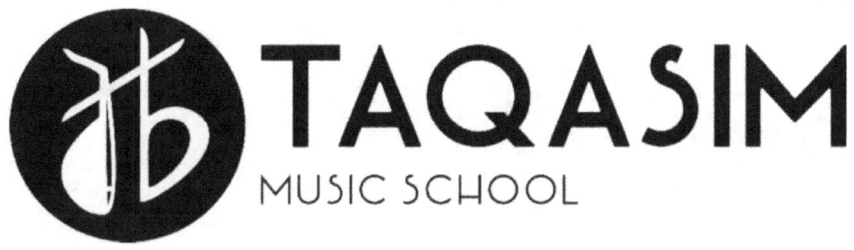

THE MUKHTAR METHOD

OUD UPPER ADVANCED

By

Ahmed Mukhtar

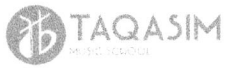

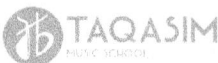

© *2019 Ahmed Mukhtar*

ISBN 978-0-244-14419-7

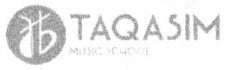

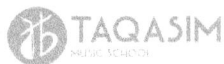

Table of Contents

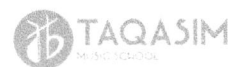

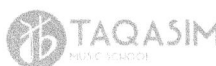

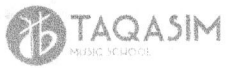

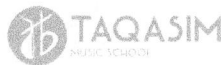

Forward

The composing of a teaching method for any musical instrument is a challenge, but the writing of a method for the Oriental Oud is, by its very nature, a monumental achievement. The Oud carries a prestigious millennial tradition stemming from Ancient Babylon, of a musical system systematically different from the Western model. It is the soul of Oriental philosophy, in the classical sense of the term, and its teaching requires such wisdom that the spirituality contained within can blossom into the limitless sophistications of *Maqam* expressionism. As with classical string instruments such as those of the string quartet, the Oud is fretless, therefore free from the limitations of tonality and open to a universe of modality.

This comprehensive method is progressive and covers all aspects of the Arabian musical system with two levels of theory, and a practical approach in six steps: Beginners; Upper beginners; Intermediate; Upper intermediate; Advanced and Upper advanced.
The method, at all levels, introduces a concept unique to Oriental music, the *rouhiyyah*, by which musicians, through the music they play, reach a state of spiritual enlightenment which is at the core of the Maqamian expression.

During my working life as an Orientalist, I have met with the few illustrious Oud Masters. With them we had endless discussions on method, on interpretation, but it is only with the Maestro Ahmed Mukhtar that I have found a true dedication to the teaching of the instrument. His method applies rigor with a gentle touch. Through his punctilious method Ahmed Mukhtar has adapted the traditional methods to the requirements of Western neophytes and thus contributed to a Western understanding of the Oriental thought.

For these reasons, and many more, I can but only give my sincere and heartfelt congratulations to Maestro Ahmed Mukhtar's excellence not only as a remarkable soloist but also as a dedicated educator in one of its most complex forms which is the art of the Oud.

Richard Dumbrill
December 2018

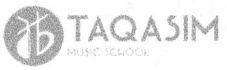

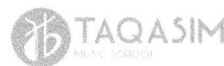

Acknowledgements

The Mukhtar Method curriculum started as a research project as part of my studies at SOAS while earning an MA in Music Performance in 2004. The Beginner level curriculum was further developed in 2009 and used to teach my private oud students as well as those I taught at SOAS. One year later, the Taqasim Music School was established, and the Oud Beginner book was used as the core material for the course. In 2013, the Oud Upper Beginner Book was written and used. Over the years, other books were developed (and continue to be developed) to create the full series. Much time and effort has been spent in the research and development stages of this teaching method.

The completion of this book was made possible by the contributions of many. I would like to offer a heartfelt thank you to:

Ahmed Beyh,
for the book cover photography.

Ruba Hillawi,
for contributing to the completion of all books in the series by editing their content, and layout.

Emma Vazquez,
for designing the Taqasim Music School logo.

Seung Hee Ko (Erika),
for designing the book covers for the entire Mukhtar Method series.

Ahmed Mukhtar

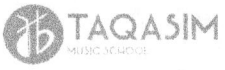

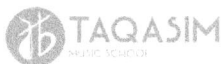

Introduction

This book has been written for learners who know most technical and theoretical techniques used on the oud. Such skills include: playing accurately in all three positions; playing a maqam or a song in only the 2nd or 3rd positions; using ornamentation in the 2nd position and sometimes the 3rd; to know *maqam* transpositions from main notes and open strings; and understanding different kinds of technical transpositions.

In this book, most of the pieces studied are very well-known master pieces. A masterpiece is a piece of music that combines high technique with a high level of expressing the feeling, spirit and soul of the music being played. This feeling is known as *rouhiyyah* in Arabic. When playing a master piece, the player is expected to shift between positions and use a complex combination of finger techniques and positions. Many pieces modulate from one *maqam* to another quite frequently. Listening to the pieces being played will help guide your progress.

The material in this book will guide you through these masterpieces and simplify the way they are played to help you progress using correct playing technique, position and *risha*. Remember to begin playing the pieces provided at different speeds, beginning at a slower pace before picking up the tempo. Also, playing the same piece at different tempos will progress technique, risha control and the ability to add ornamentation effectively. Transposing the pieces to different keys will also allow an opportunity to apply different techniques with changed finger positions and provide a different set of oranmentative possibilities.

At the Upper Advanced level, the ornamentation of each piece has been left out. At this level, a player is at the stage where he/she should be able to add their own ornamentation, experiment with the sounds of each within a piece and decide which ornamentation highlights the spirit/*rouhiyyah* of the maqam being played within each musical sentence. The is a need to embody the music in order to perform it with feeling and this can only be done if the player him/herself is able to apply ornamental patterns independently and effectively.

Here is a list of suggested ornamentations that can be applied to the masterpieces in this book: fast and slow tremolos; vibratos; qarar & jawab; dynamics; advanced *trills* (more than one *trill* per note); advanced glissando (sliding between more than one tone); and the playing of multiple ornametative patterns at once. Such combinations could be: tremolo + qarar; *trill* + tremolo; *trill* + glissando among various other combination that are open to interpretation.

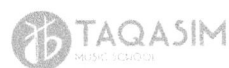

Terminology

Aqid: An Arabic musical term similar to a tetrachord/jins using 5 consecutive notes in a maqam.

Dynamics: Defines how loud or soft notes are played within a piece. Changing the volume of each note is one way of showcasing the feelings of a given *maqam*.

Glissando: "Passing all or part of the way from one note to another on the same string." **

Jins (pl. Ajnaas)/Tetrachord: The first 4 and last 4 notes in a scale.

Maqam: A scale used in Arabic music which contains 6 definitive tones and carries a specific mood and spirit.

Micro-Tone (Quarter-Tone): "An interval smaller than a semi-tone."**

Modulation: The smooth transition from one maqam to another related maqam within a given piece of music.

Transposition: The writing or performance of a composition (or scale) at a different pitch from its original (keeping the same intervals).**

Trill: An ornamentation comprised of a rapid alternation of one note and the note above it within a *maqam*.**

Leading Note: "The 7th degree of a major or minor scale, a semitone below the tonic."**

Taqasim: A term simply defined as "musical improvisation", although far more complex. The main difference is that the performer uses traditional pre-composed musical phrases linking each of those phrases using improvised lines. The phrases used can be played in a variety of ways using different ornamentation.

Tarab: A state of musical ecstasy.

Tone: The unit of measurement used in the tonal system to measure intervals between notes.
*Tonic (***Settled Note***)*: The first degree of the scale of a maqam. The maqam starts, settles and ends using this note.**

Scale: A group of intervaled notes that ascend or descend in order. This series of notes within a given octave is used to compose any given piece of music.

Secondary *Maqam*: A *maqam* that shares its first jins/tetrachord with one of the primary *maqamaat*.

Sensitive Note: A distinctive note of a scale which allows the listeners to identify/define the maqam being played.

Solfeggio: Method of vocal sight-reading.*

Vibrato: "Vibrated". An undulating, tremulous effect used on stringed instruments and voices to increase the emotional quality of the note."*

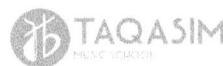

Resources

The following dictionaries have been used as references to define and/or paraphrase some of the above definitions.

* Lovelock, William. *A Student's Dictionary of Music.* G.Bell & Sons, 1979.

** Kennedy, Michael, Tim Rutherford-Johnson, and Joyce Kennedy. *The Oxford Dictionary of Music.* OUP Oxford, 2013.

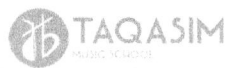

Reading Resources

Below is a list of reliable resources to read for extra information about the history of Arabic music and the Oud.

English Resources

Farmer, Henry George. *A History of Arabian Music to the XIIIth Century*. Luzac, 1929.
The Arabian Influence on Musical Theory. H. Reeves, 1925.

Racy, Ali Jihad. *Making Music in the Arab World : The Culture and Artistry of Ṭarab /*. Cambridge Middle East Studies ; Cambridge ; New York : Cambridge University Press, 2003.

Sawa, George Dimitri. *Music Performance Practice in the Early c Abbasid Era 132-320 AH / 750-932 AD*. 01 edition. Toronto, Ont., Canada: Pontifical Institute of Mediaeval Studies, 1989.

Shiloah, Amnon. *Music in the World of Islam: A Socio-Cultural Study*. Wayne State University Press, 2001.

Touma, H. H. *The Music of the Arabs /*. New expd. ed. Portland, OR : Amadeus Press, 1996.

Arabic Resources

أنور, صبحي، رشيد. تاريخ العود. دار علاء الدين، 1999

تاريخ الموسيقى العربية. مؤسسة باقاريا، 2000.

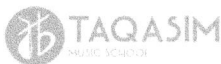

Arabic Musical Forms

Samaa'i

The *samaa'i* is typically made of four sections and a refrain. A section is referred to as a *khanah (khanat pl.)* and the refrain is called *taslim*. A key feature of a *samaa'i* is that each *khanah* is composed using a different *maqam*. The first *khanah* and the *taslim* share a *maqam*, while the 2nd, 3rd and 4th *khanat* are composed using different *maqamat*. The first three *khanat* are written using the *rhythm known as Samaa'i Thaqil*, or 10/8 time, while the fourth is written at an up-beat pace of 3/4 or 6/8 time known as *Samaa'i Darij*.

Longa

The *Longa* is an instrumental form written using a 2/4 time signature and is made of several *khanat*. Each *khanah* followed by a *taslim*. However, that the last *khanah* is usually written in 3/4 time. A *longa* is quite lively and is played at high tempos.

Tahmilah

The *tahmilah* is an instrumental piece played using alternating sections played by an ensemble as well as solo instruments. The parts played by the ensemble are relatively fixed compositions, whereas the solos are mostly improvised, providing plenty of room for individual expression.

Doulab

A *doulab* is a short, instrumental prelude normally performed in unison by an ensemble. Its purpose is to introduce the audience to the maqam that will be played in the coming piece of music. A doulab achieves this by presenting the basic structure and mood of a given *maqam* prior to presenting it elaborately in a coming piece of music and/or song.

Taqasim

Taqasim refers to pieces that are semi-improvised forms and are usually without rhythmic accompaniment. A *maqsoum* (sl.) is meant to demonstrate the structure of a particular *maqam* and its relation to other *maqamaat*. Its performance is a highly skilled art and relies on an intimate knowledge of the structure of the different *maqamaat* and their interrelation. When performing, an artist will follow the general flow of a *maqam*, while emphasizing important tones and using key melodic phrases while modulating to several related *maqamaat*.

Sirto

A *sirto* is similar to the *longa* in that it is usually played in 2/4 or 4/4 time. Some sirtos combine different time signatures such as 2/4 and 7/8 in the same piece.

Free-style Piece

This type of composition has been known in Arabic music since the beginning of the 20th century. It usually contains 2 or 3 movements played in the order of A, B, A, C. In this book the piece titled *Sulaf* is one such example.

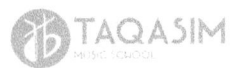

Left Hand Positions (fingers)

There are several positions on the oud. In each position, every string uses all four fingers to cover the entire span of that position.

Position changes are indicated within the tablature lines using the abbreviation "pos....." followed by the position numbers "1", "2" or "3"

The first, second and third positions of the left hand are illustrated here:

1) In the **1ˢᵗ position**, the thumb of the left hand rests on the neck of the oud just below where the neck and the peg box meet. The thumb needs to remain stationary.

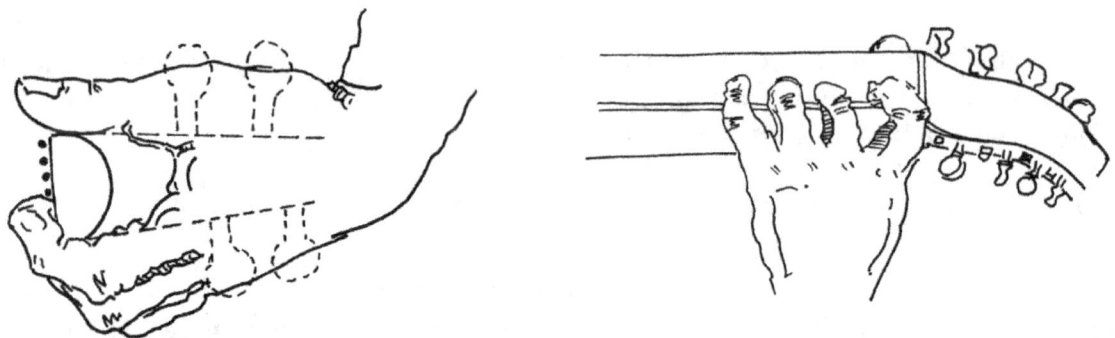

2) In the **2ⁿᵈ position**, the thumb slides approximately half way down the neck of the Oud. The same fingering technique is used.

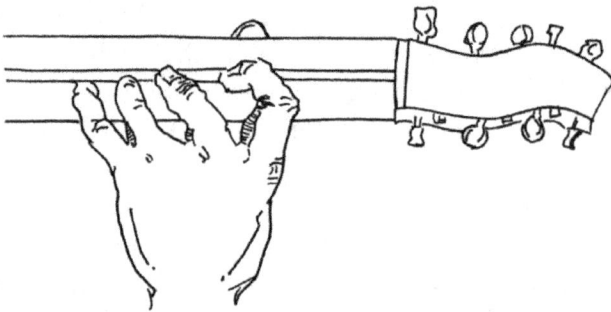

3) In the **3ʳᵈ position**, the thumb slides further down the neck of the Oud resting where the neck meets the body. The same fingering technique is used.

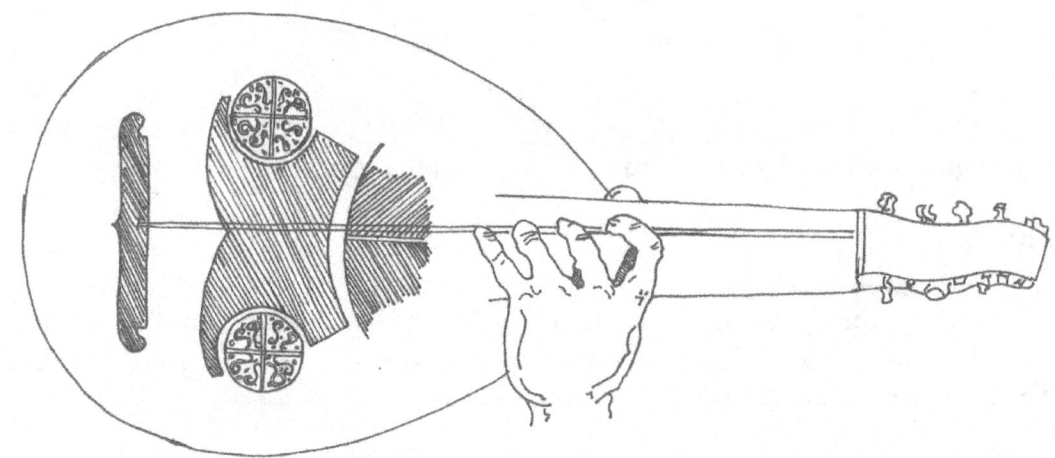

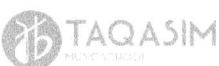

Maqamaat - 3 Octaves & 3 Positions

The *maqam* scales below are written in 3 octaves using all three positions on the oud. The curved line drawn on each of the scales indicates where the scale in played in the 3rd position on one string.

Some *maqamaat* such as *Nahawand*, change on the descending scale. Those note changes are shown in brackets next to the altered note.

Remember that quarter-tones are very sensitive. Pay attention to where these notes change in descending scales, such as in *Rast*. The tabs written will guide you to play the tones accurately.

Ajam Fa – 3 octaves

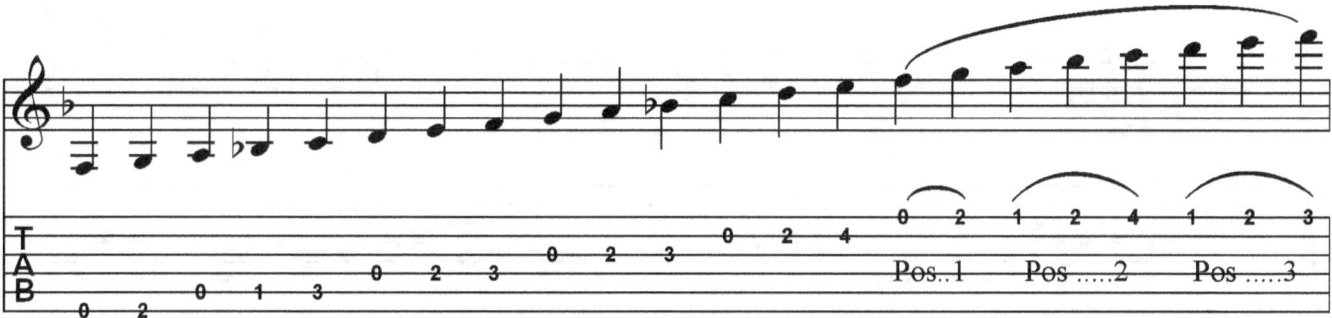

Nahawand Fa – 3 octaves

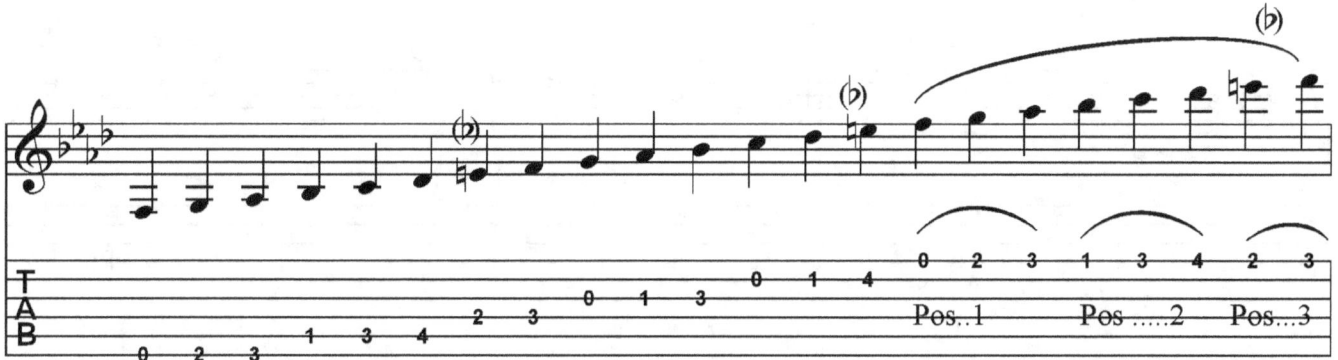

Kurd Fa – 3 octaves

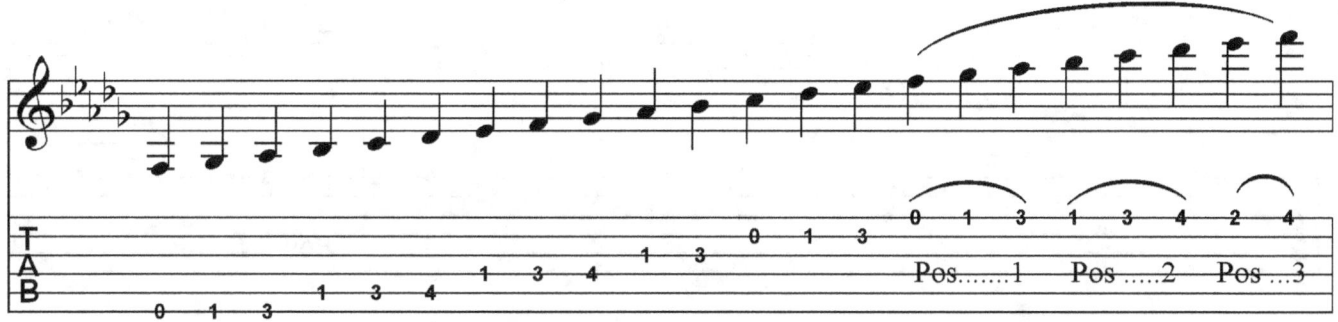

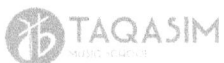

Hijaz Fa – 3 octaves

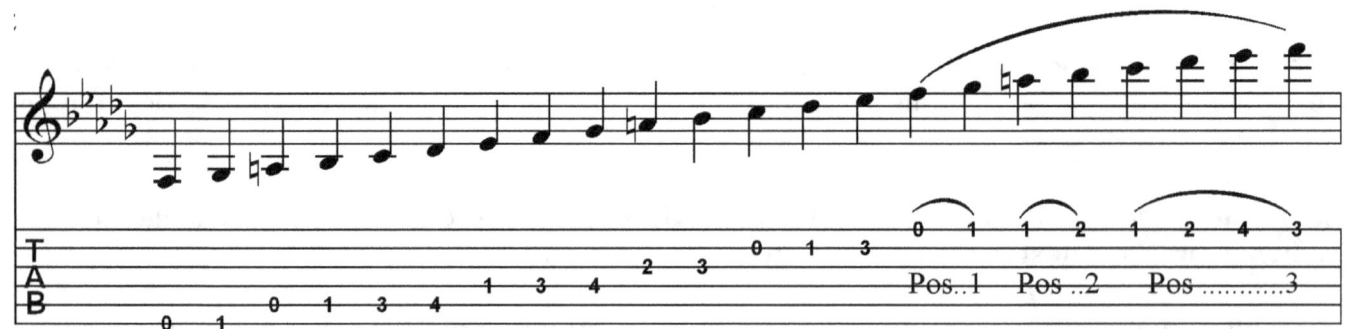

Bayat Fa- 3 octaves

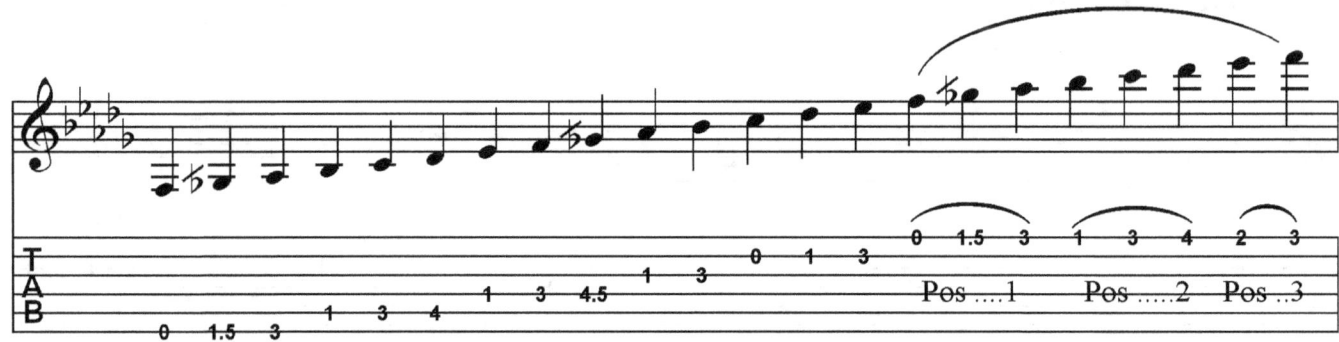

Saba Fa – 3 octaves

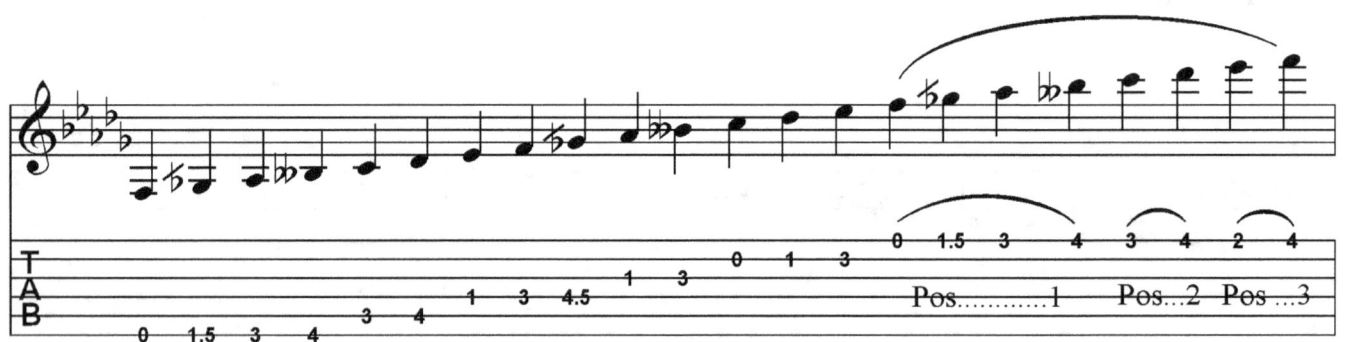

Rast Fa – 3 octaves

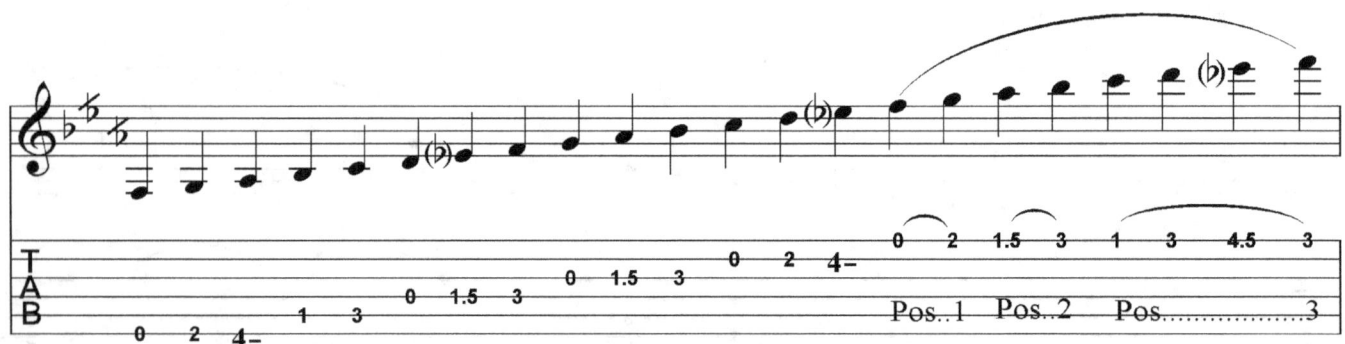

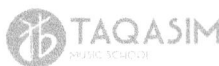

Bayat Sol – 3 octaves

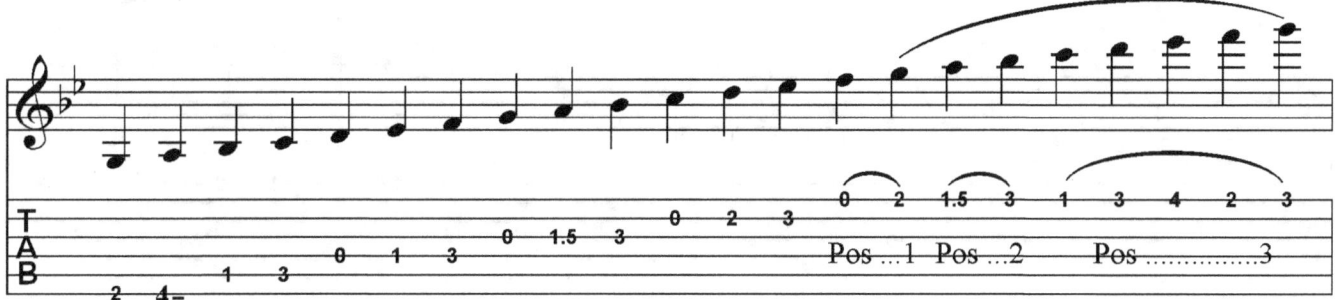

Kurd Sol – 3 octaves

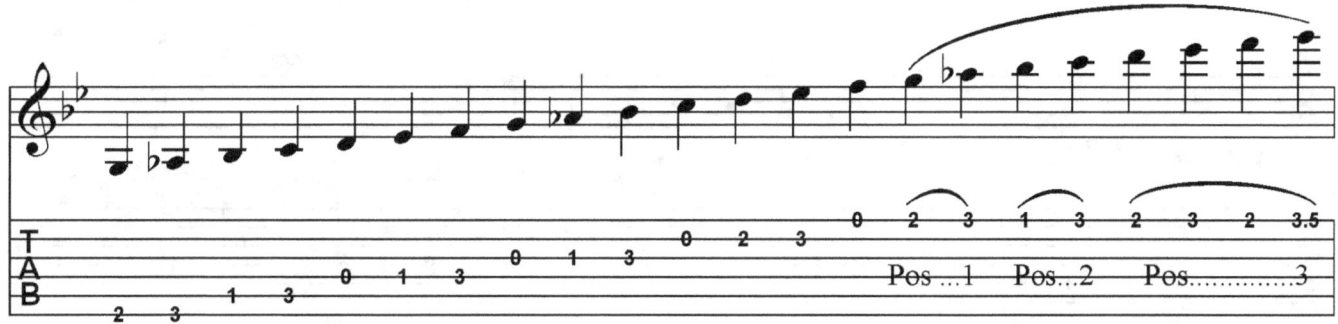

Nahawand Sol – 3 octaves

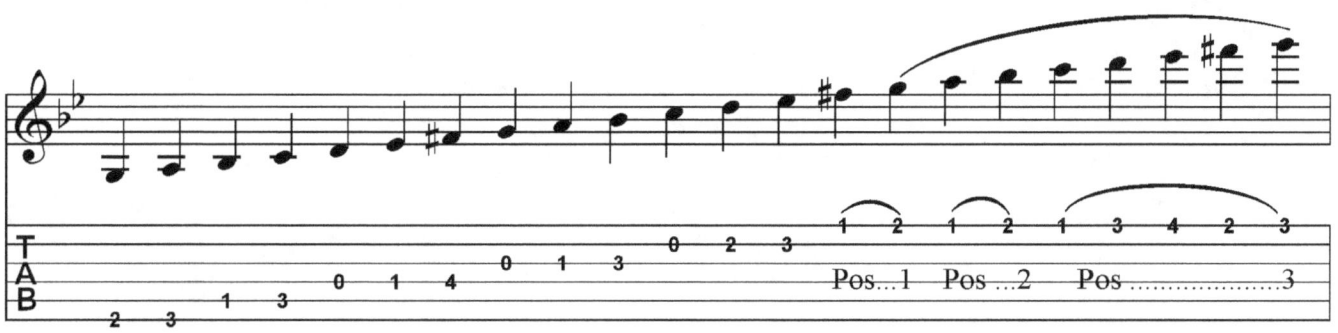

Hijaz Sol – 3 octaves

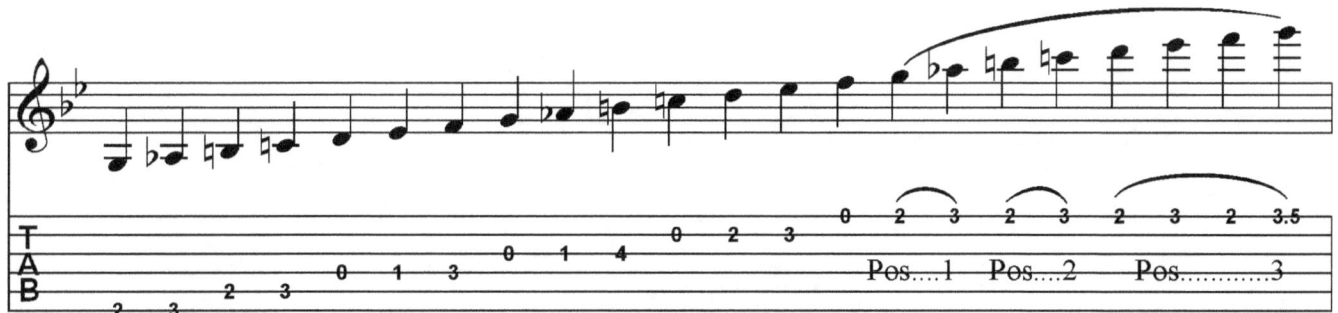

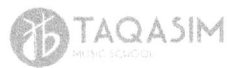

Saba Sol – 3 octaves

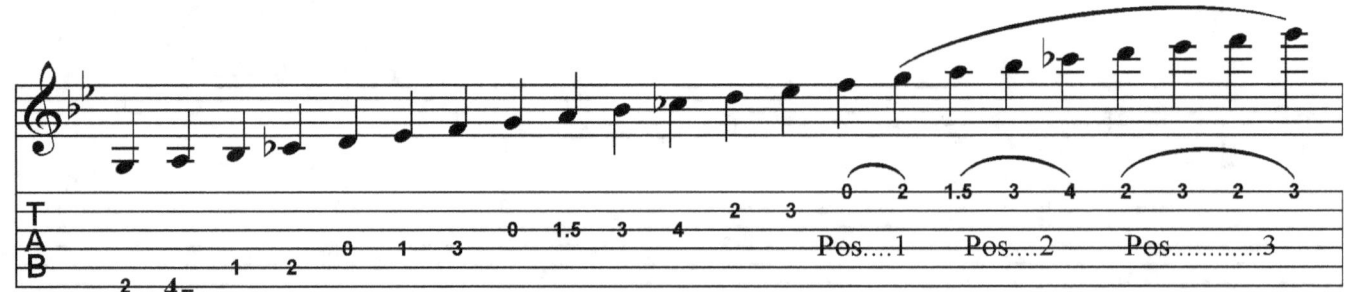

Huzam Fa half-sharp – 3 octaves

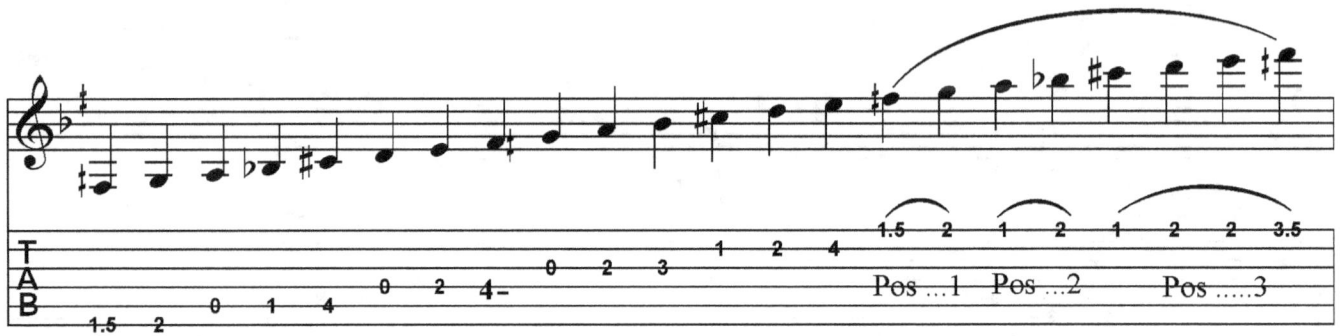

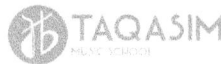

Transposed Maqamaat – 2 octaves & 3 positions

These *maqam* scales are transposed from different keys and written in 2 octaves. Notice that the second octave of each *maqam* scale is played using all 3 positions on one string.

Remember to take note of the *maqam* scales that change on the descending scale.

Practicing these *maqam* scales regularly, accurately, and with the use of a variety of simple and complex risha techniques and at different speeds will significantly help with the progression of your playing. Using these scales as warm-up exercises will help you begin to become familiar with playing in all three positions on the 4th, 5th and 6th strings.

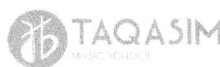

Maqam Ajam

Ajam Fa – 3 Positions on the 6th String

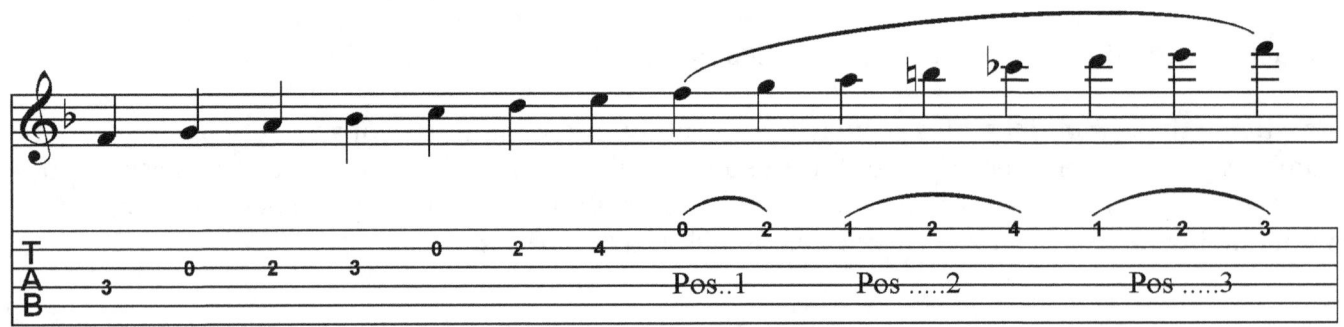

Ajam Do – 3 Positions on the 5th String

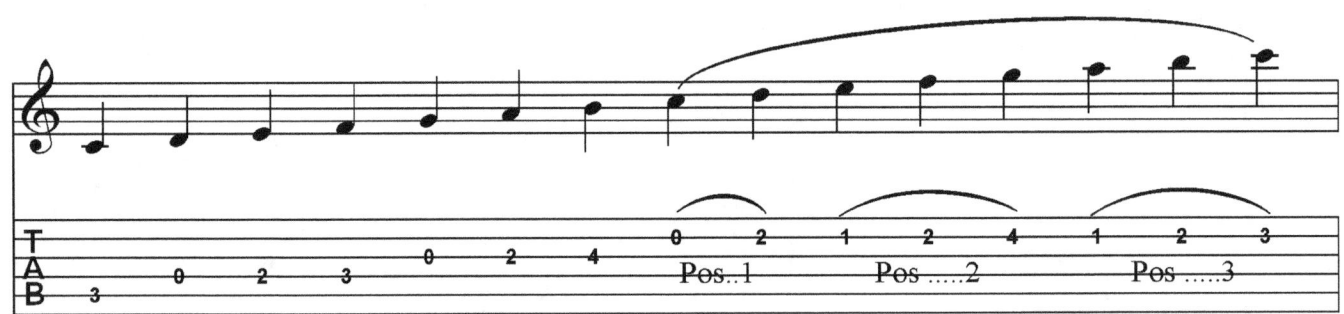

Ajam Sol – 3 Positions on the 4th String

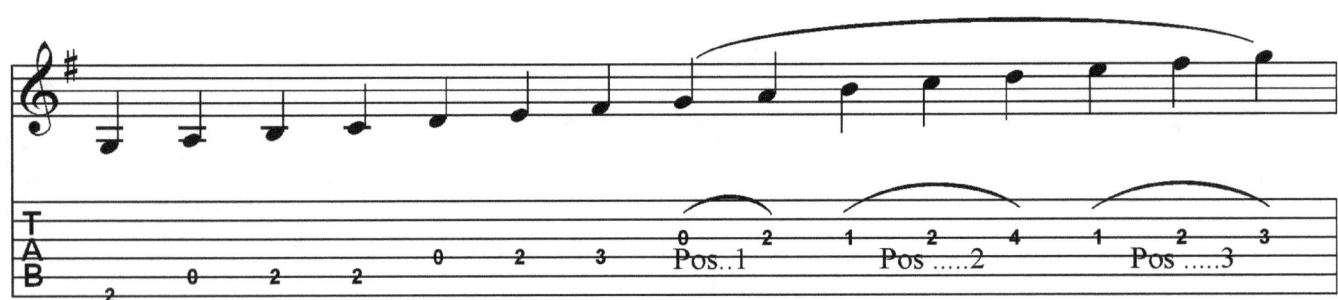

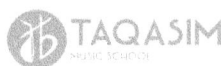

Maqam Nahawand

Nahawand Fa – 3 Positions on the 6ᵗʰ String

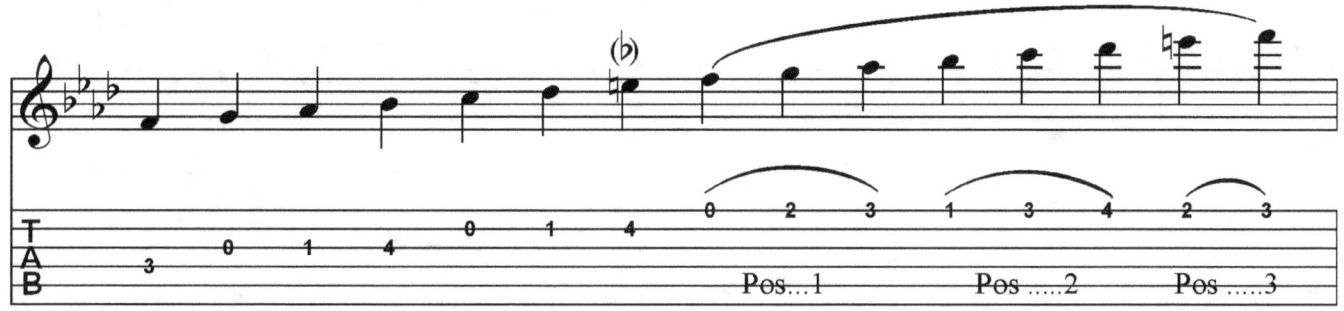

Nahawand Do – 3 Positions on the 5ᵗʰ String

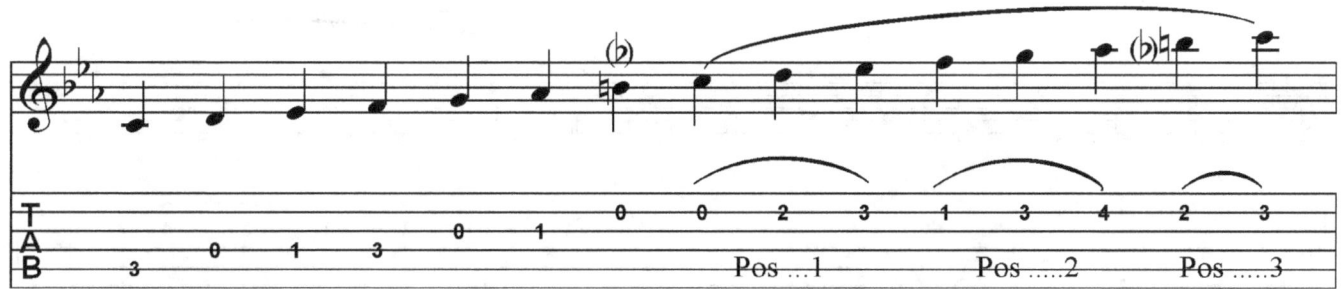

Nahawand Sol – 3 Positions on the 4ᵗʰ String

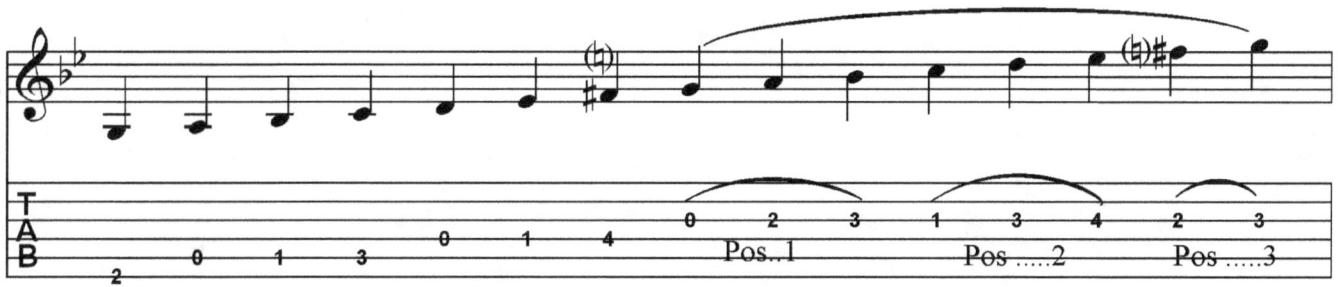

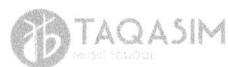

Maqam Hijaz

Hijaz Sol – 3 Positions on the 4th String

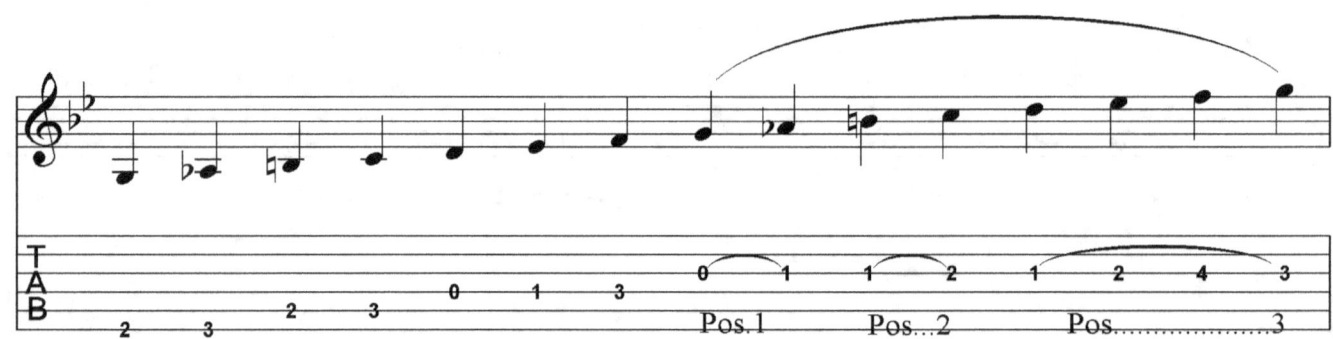

Hijaz Do – 3 Positions on the 5th String

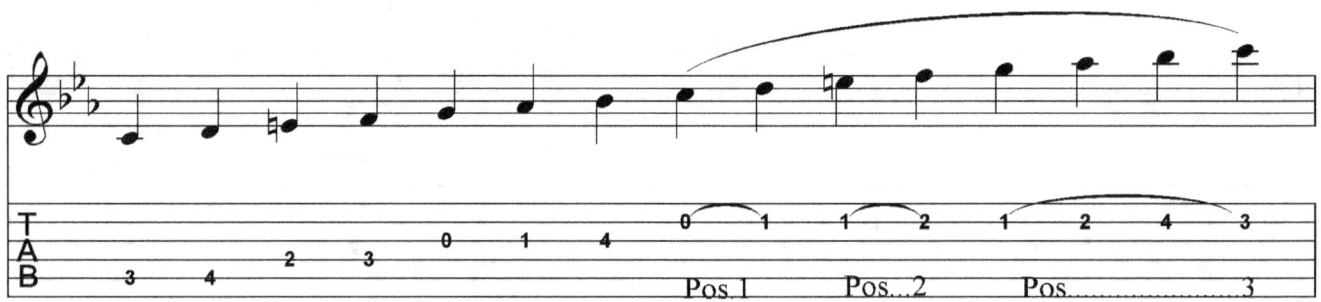

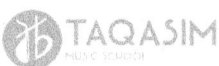

Maqam Kurd

Kurd Sol – 3 Positions on the 6th String

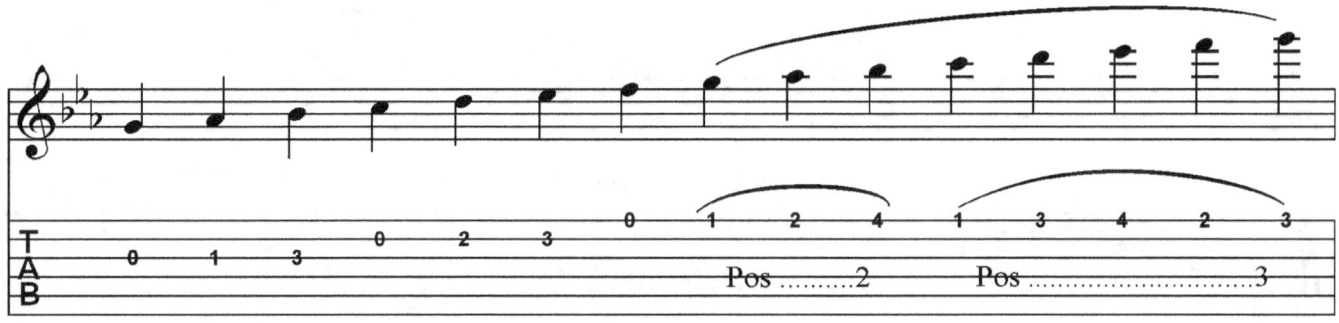

Kurd Re – 3 Positions on the 5th String

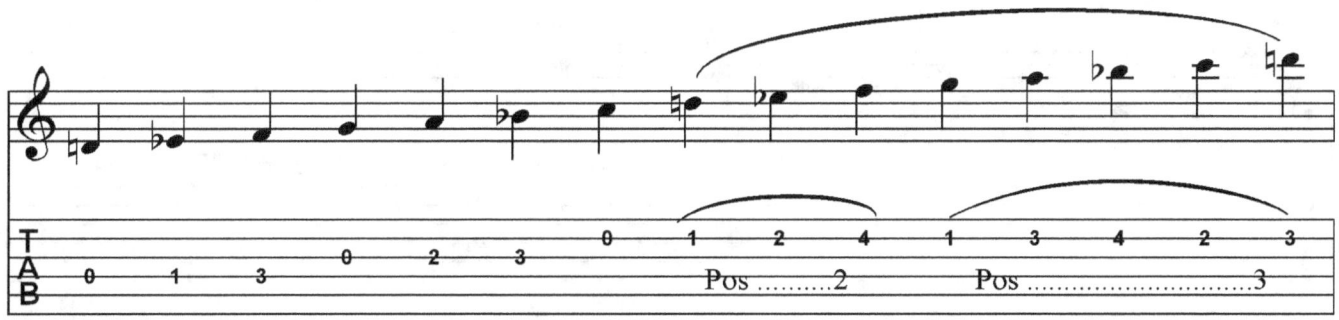

Kurd La – 3 Positions on the 4th String

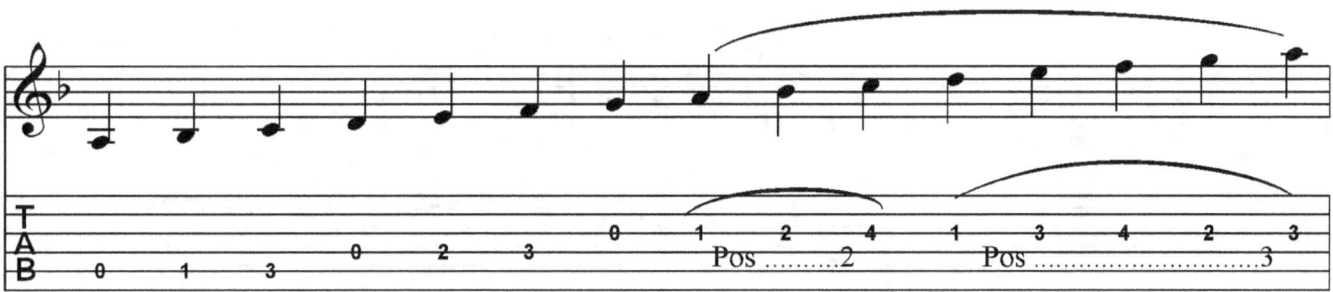

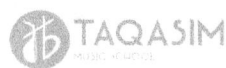

Maqam Rast

Rast Fa – 3 Positions on the 6th String

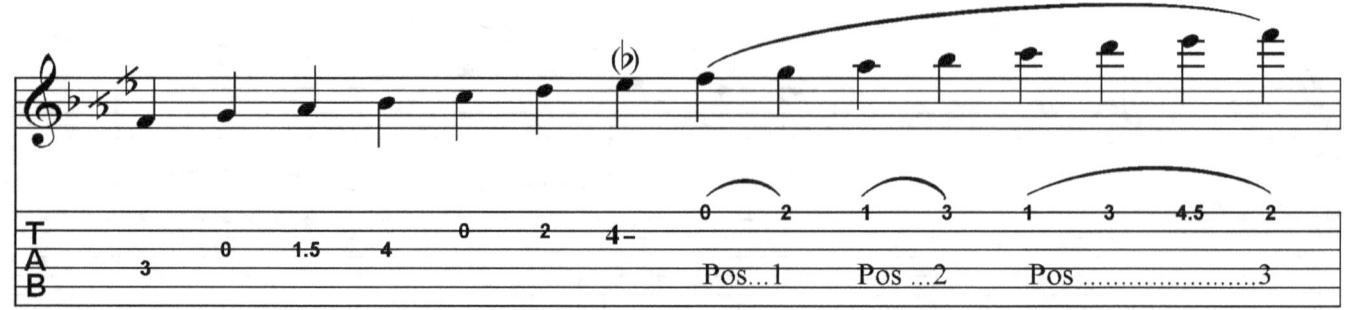

Rast Do – 3 Positions on 5thString

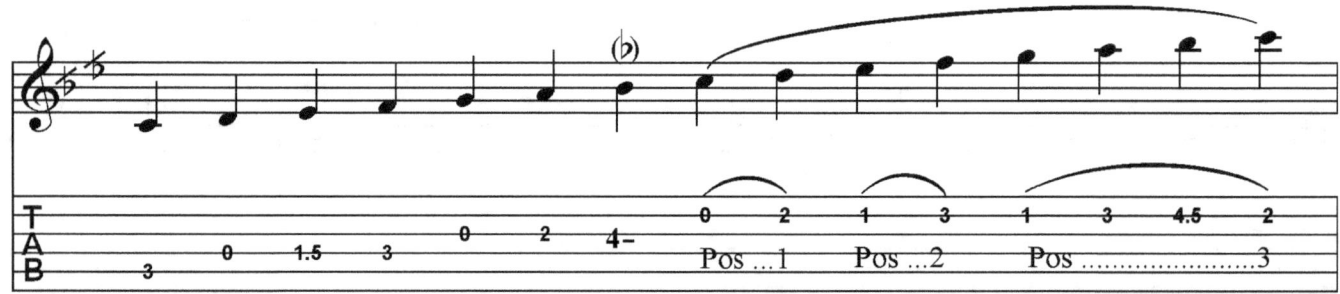

Rast Sol – 3 Positions on the 4th String

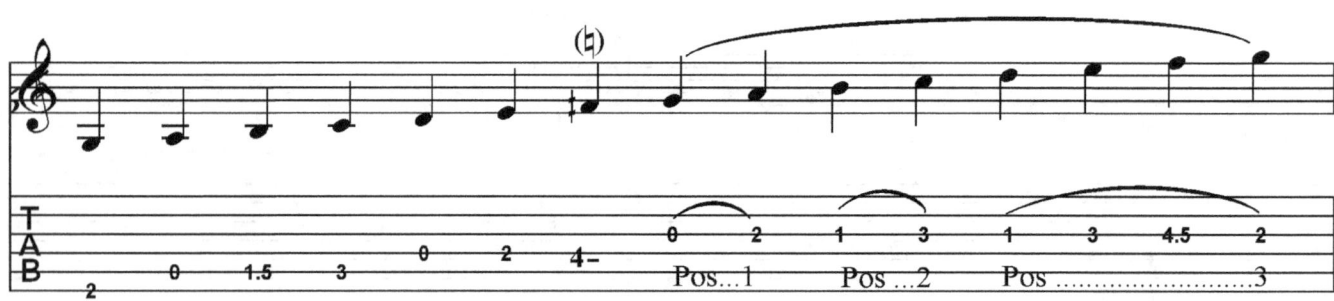

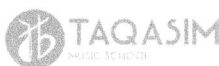

Maqam Bayat

Bayat Sol – 3 Positions on the 6th String

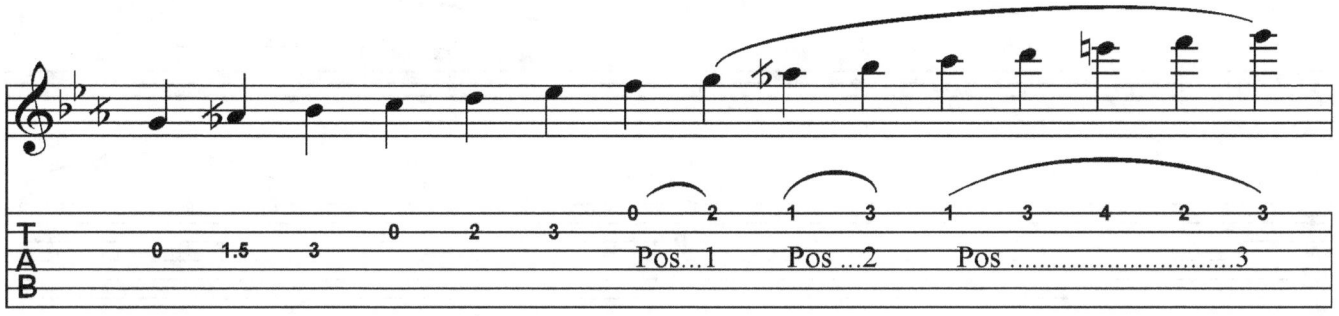

Bayat Re – 3 Positions on the 5th String

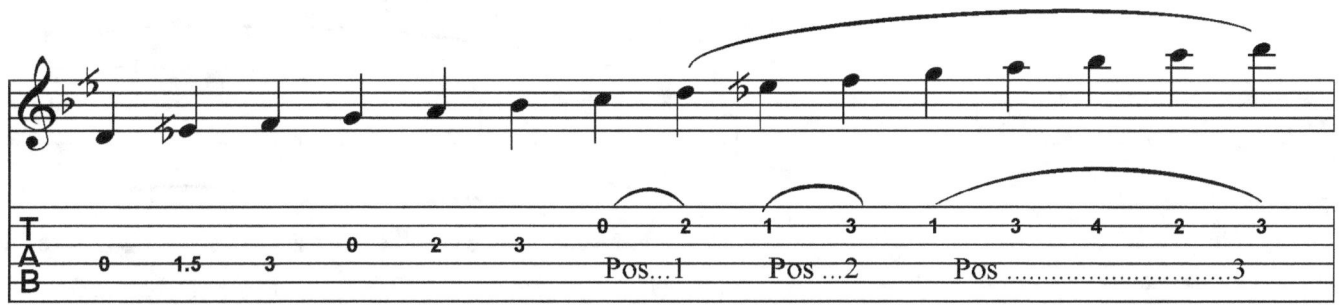

Bayat La – 3 Positions on 4th String

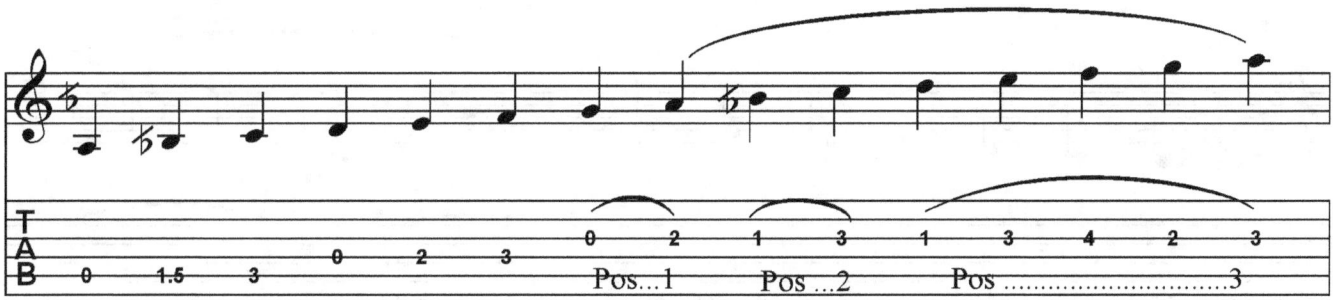

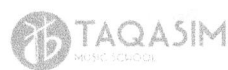

Maqam Saba

Saba Sol – 3 Positions on the 6th String

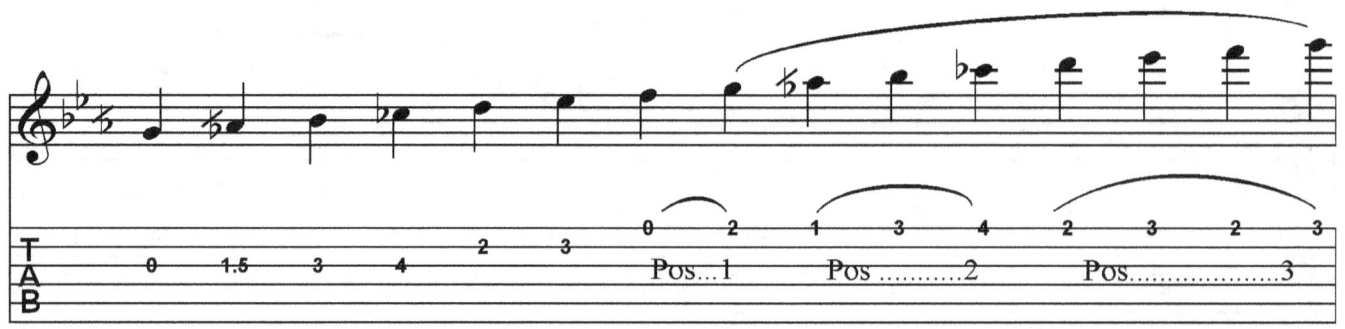

Saba Re – 3 Positions on the 5th String

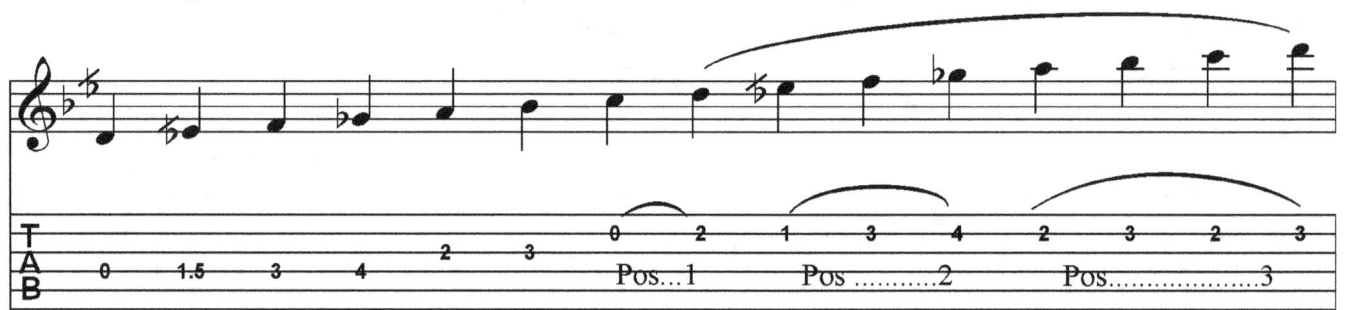

Saba La – 3 Positions on the 4th String

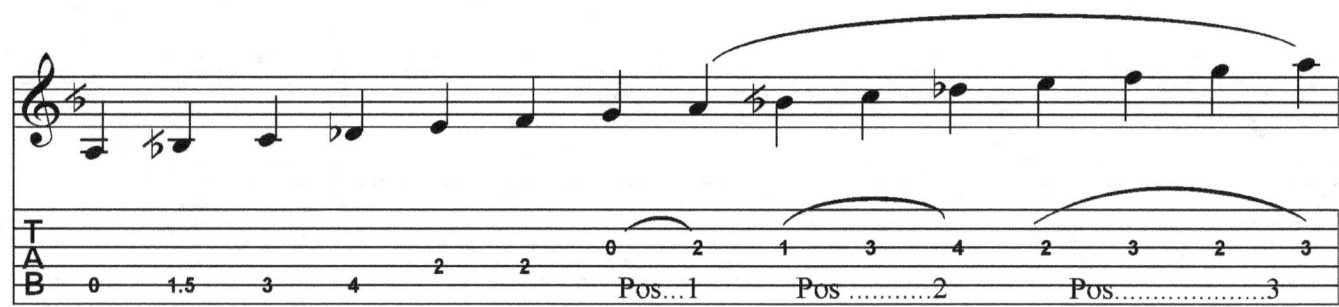

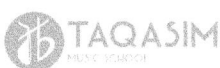

Maqam Huzam

Huzam La-half *bimol* – 3 Positions on the 6th String

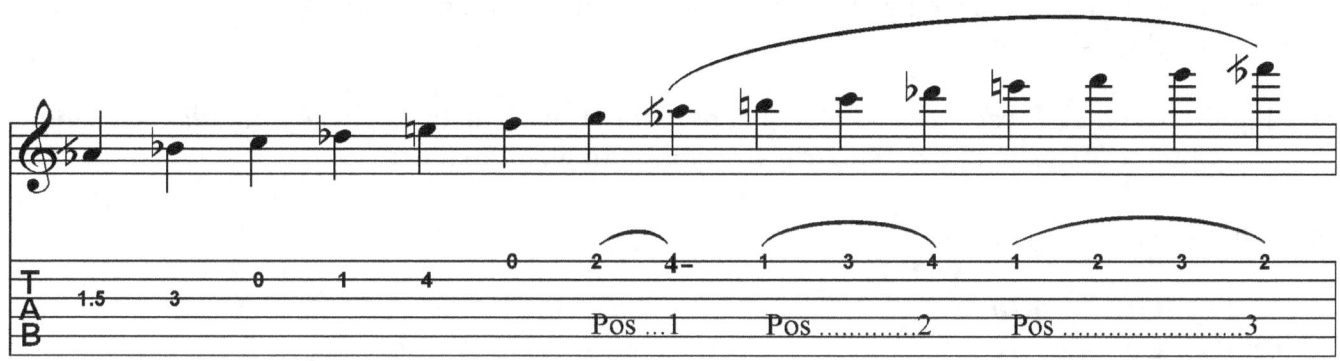

Huzam Mi half-*bimol* – 3 Positions on the 5th String

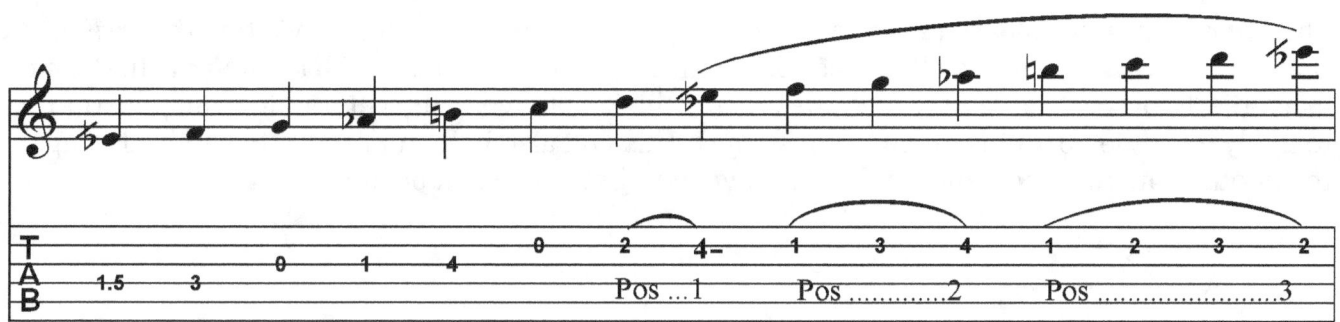

Huzam Si half-*bimol* – 3 Positions on the 4th String

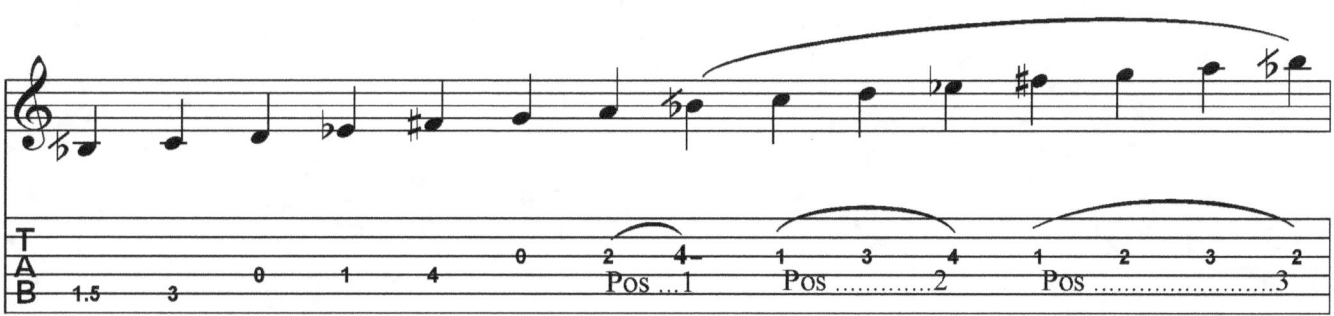

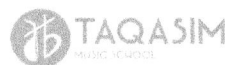

Samaaí Bayat Qadim: played in the second octave

Samaa'i Bayat Qadim is usually played in the first octave and using the first position. At the Upper Advanced level, the full piece needs to be played in the 2nd octave using whichever position is required to play accurately.

It is highly advised to practice the below list of *maqam* scales using a variety of *risha* techniques while maintaining tonal precision before attempting to play the piece.

Maqamaat to practice:

- *Bayat* Re – 2 octaves
- *Rast* Do – 2 octaves
- *Hijaz* Re – 2 octaves
- *Saba* Re – 2 octaves

The *samaa'i* form usually requires a player to repeat each *khanah* before revisiting the *taslim*. One way of practicing to play this piece using the 2nd octave is to play each *khanah* the first time using the 1st octave and to play the repeat using the 2nd octave. This will provide an opportunity to apply multiple positions on different strings. This will also help in progressing your playing technique, note precision and fluidity of movement between each position.

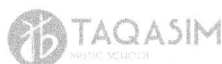

Samaa'i Bayat Qadim – Second Octave

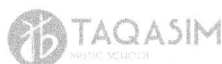

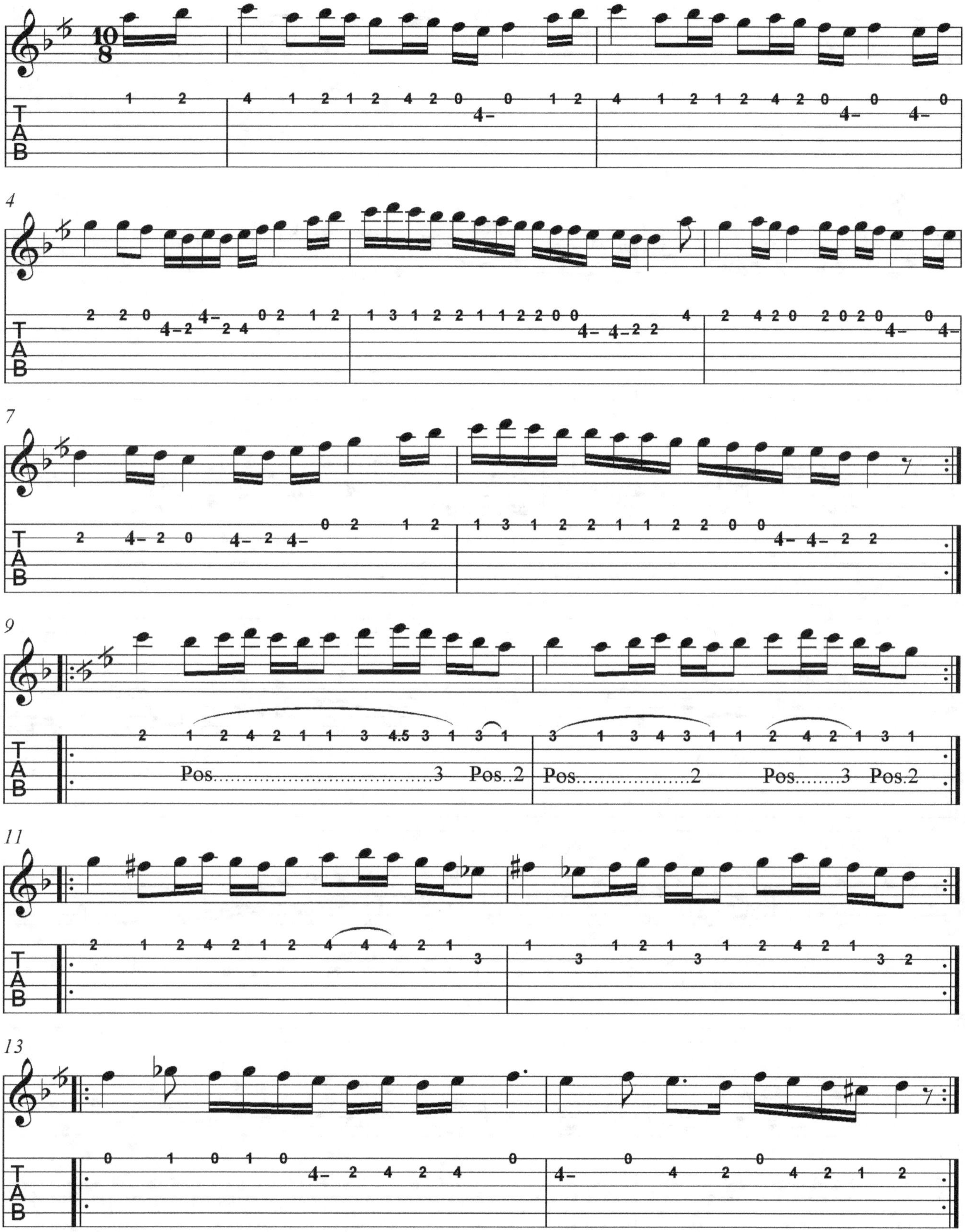

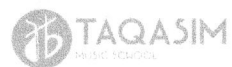

Samaa'i Bayat Qadim – 1st & 2nd **Octaves**

This piece needs to be practiced as written below. One khanah should be played on the 1st octave and its repeat in the 2nd octave.

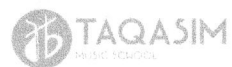

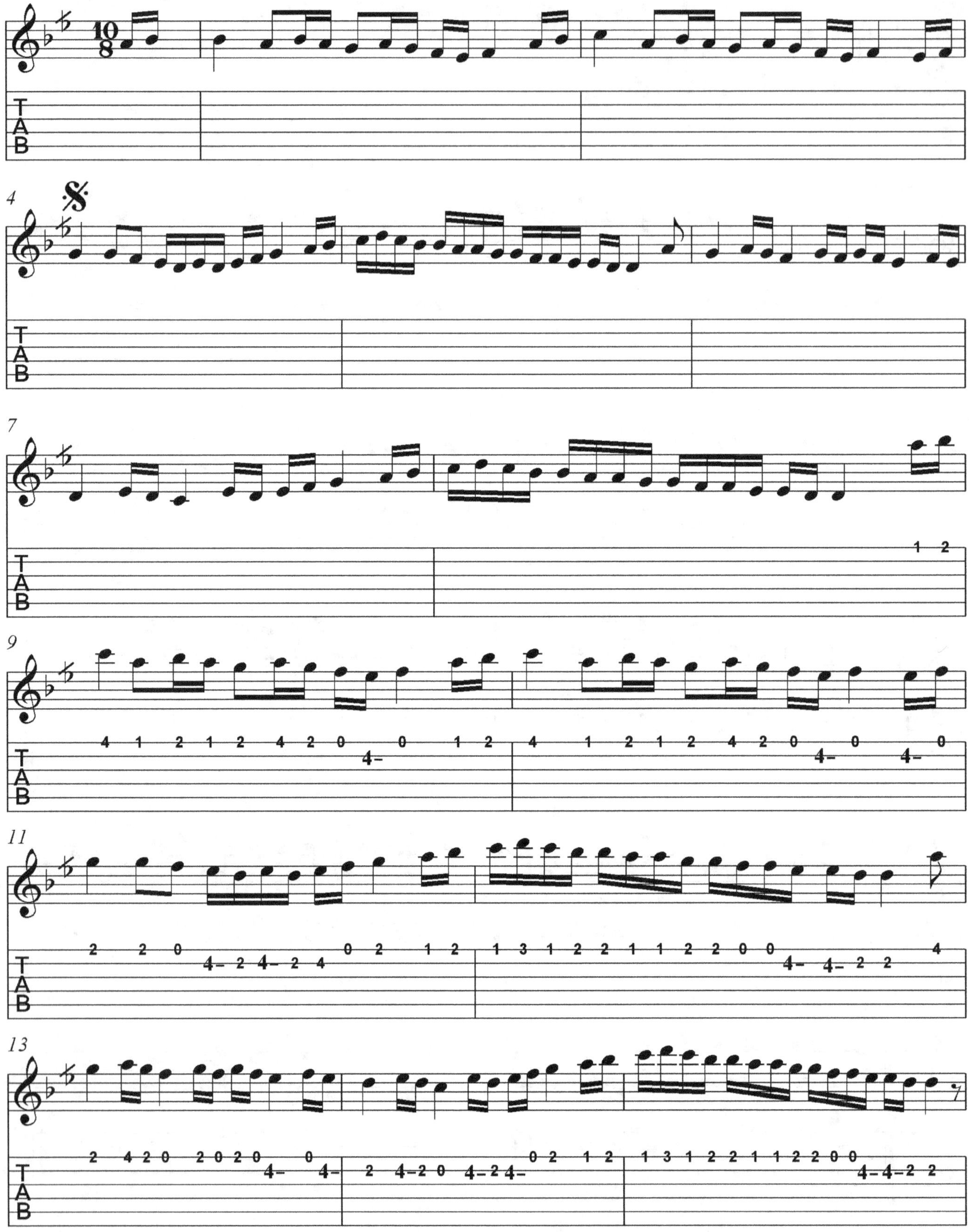

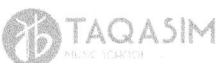

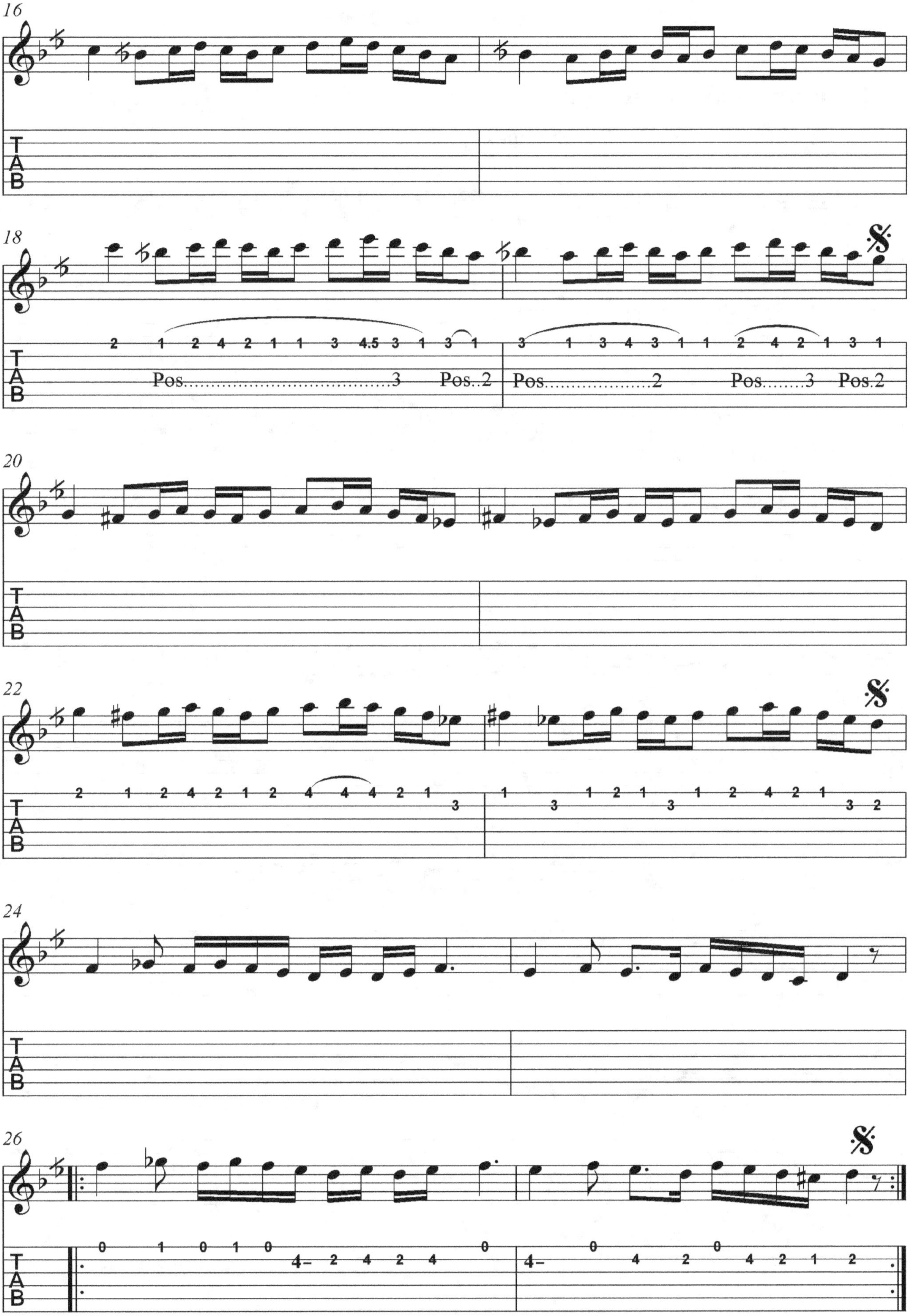

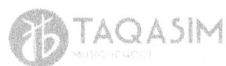

Etudes & Exercises

3rd Position *Etude* – A. Mukhtar

This etude will help progress *trill* techniques.

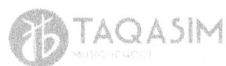

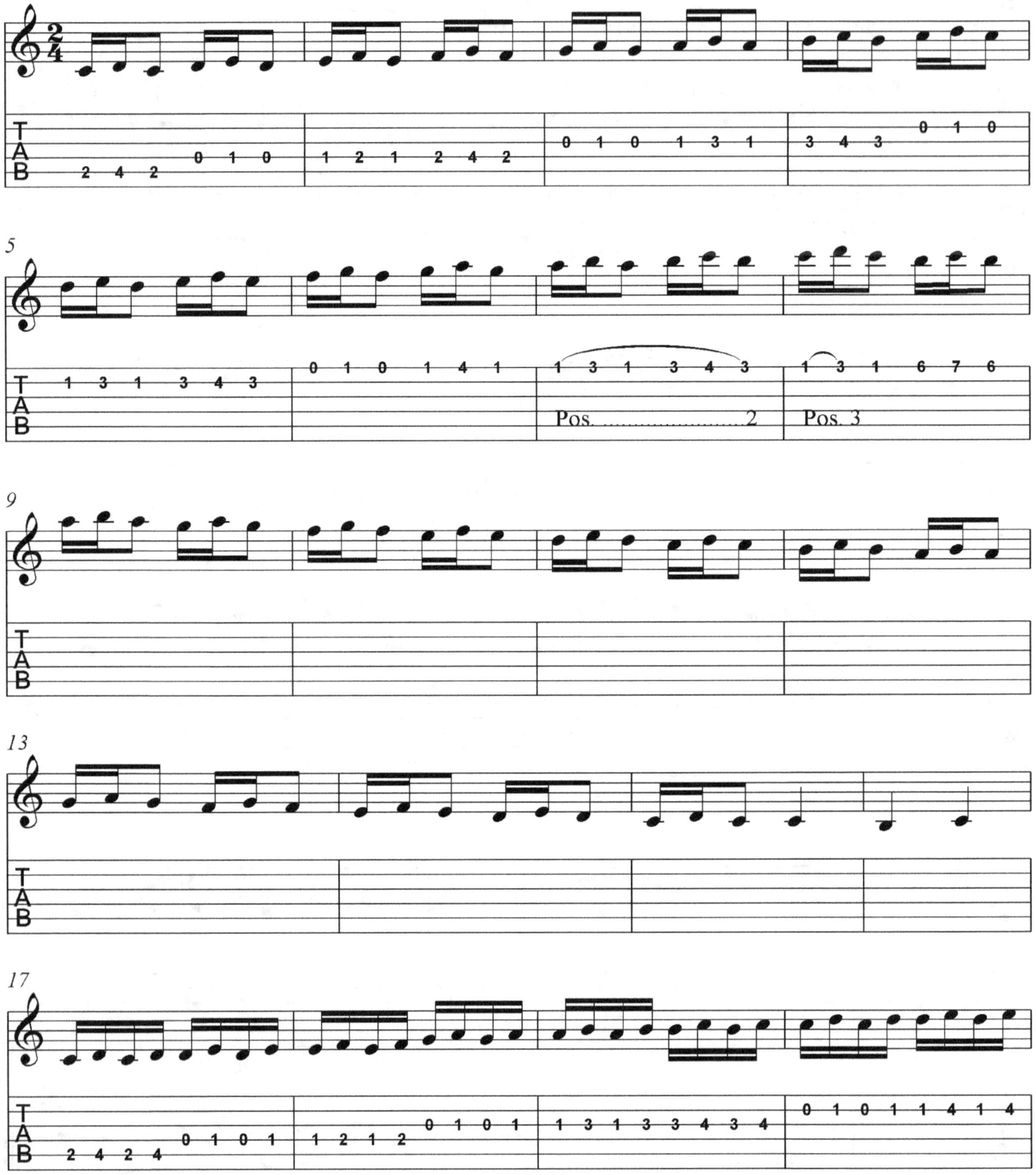

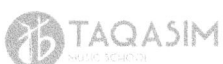

21

```
T   3 — 4 — 3 — 4    0 — 1 — 0 — 1    1 — 3 — 1 — 3    3 — 1 — 3    3 — 4 — 3 — 4 — 1 — 3 — 1 — 3
A
B
```

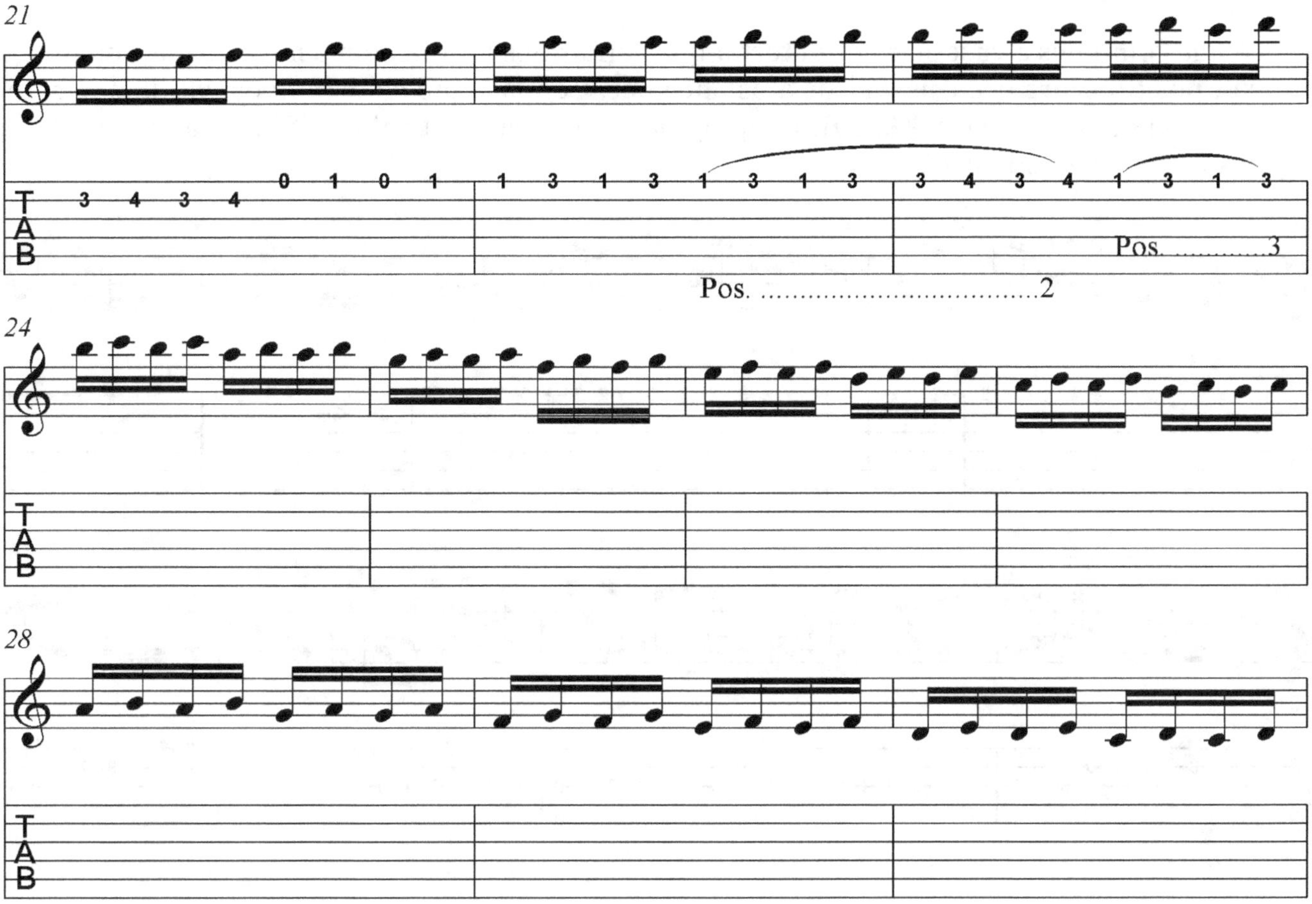

Pos. 2

Pos. 3

24

```
T
A
B
```

28

```
T
A
B
```

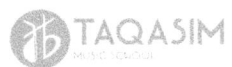

Etude – Sharif M. Haider

This *etude* combines a vast number of techniques and skills that need mastery. A combination of difficult positions are used, as well as a balance between fast and slow tempos within a bar; the playing of chords (see bars 9 & 10); jumping between strings; triplet patterns; and combining triplets with *qarar* and *jawab*.

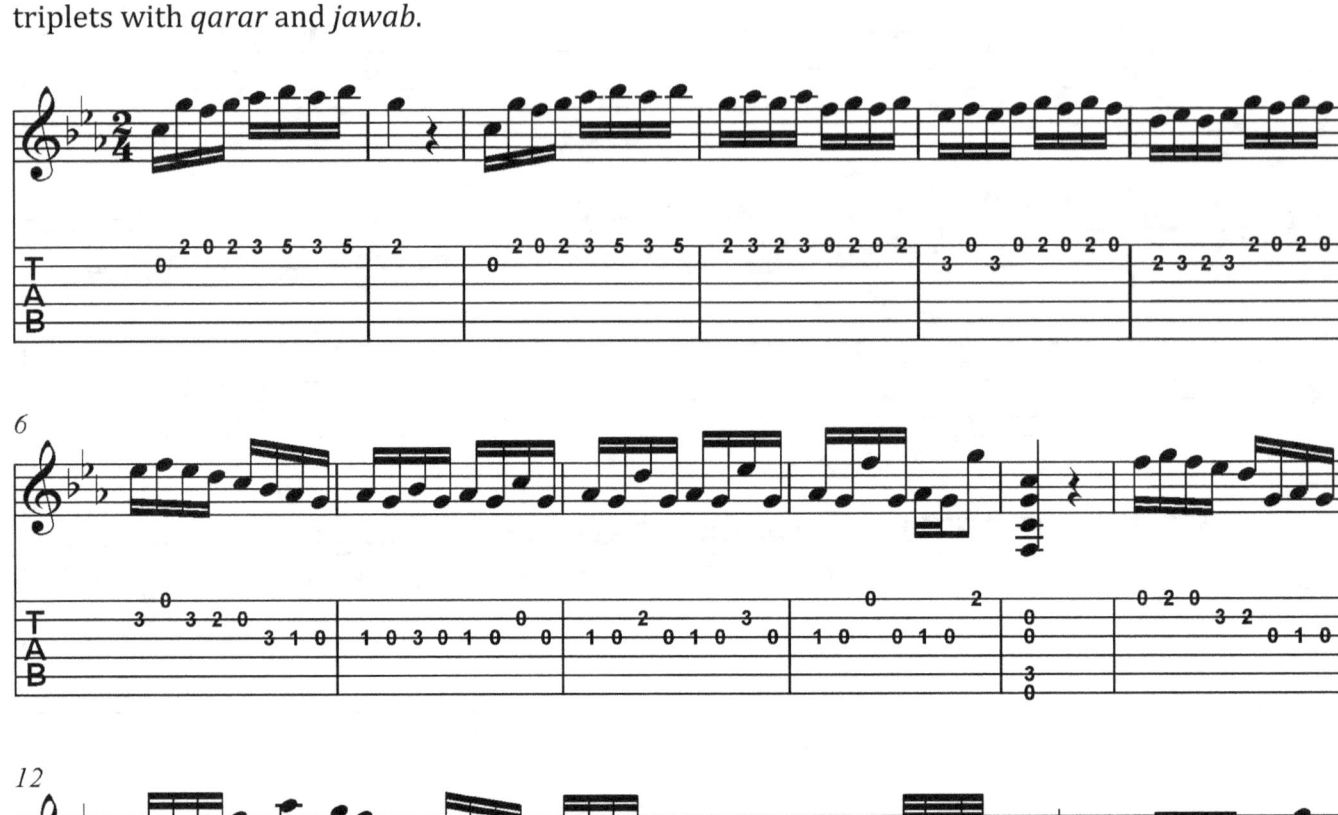

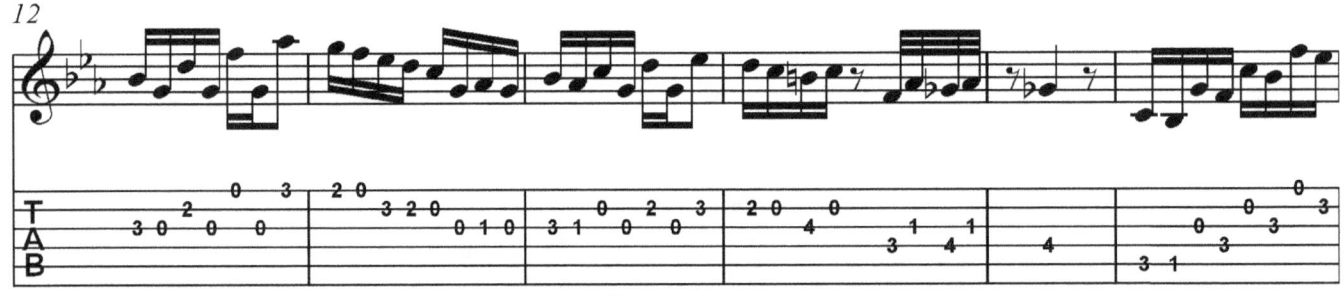

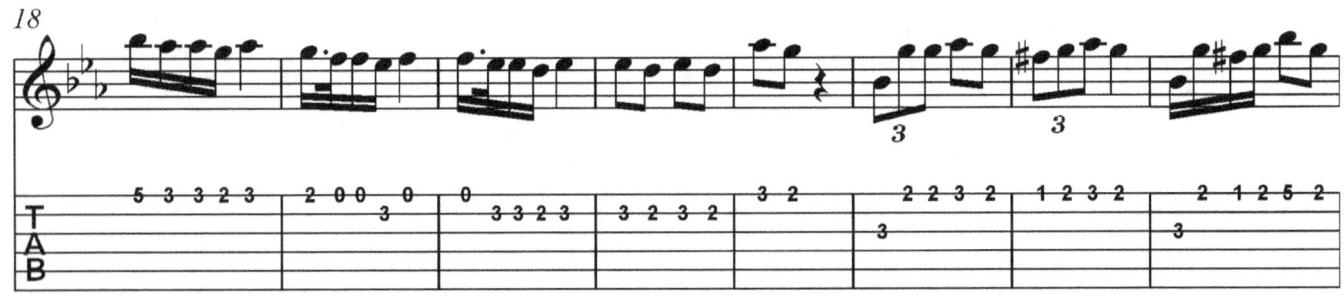

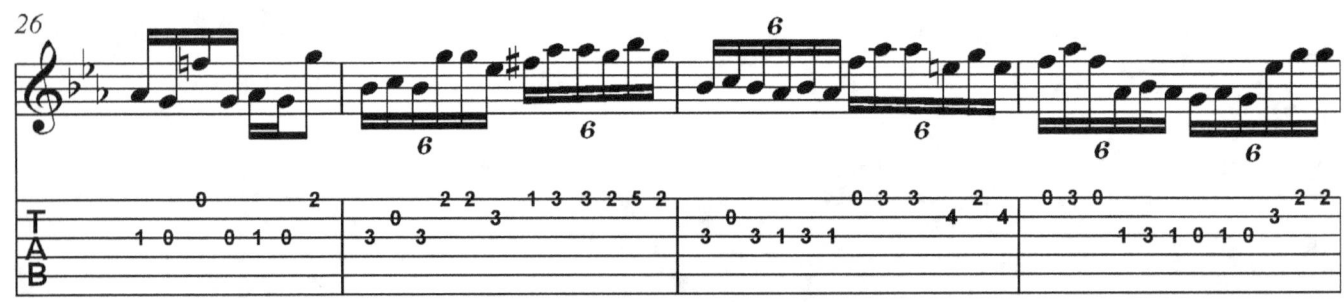

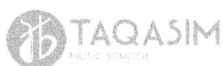

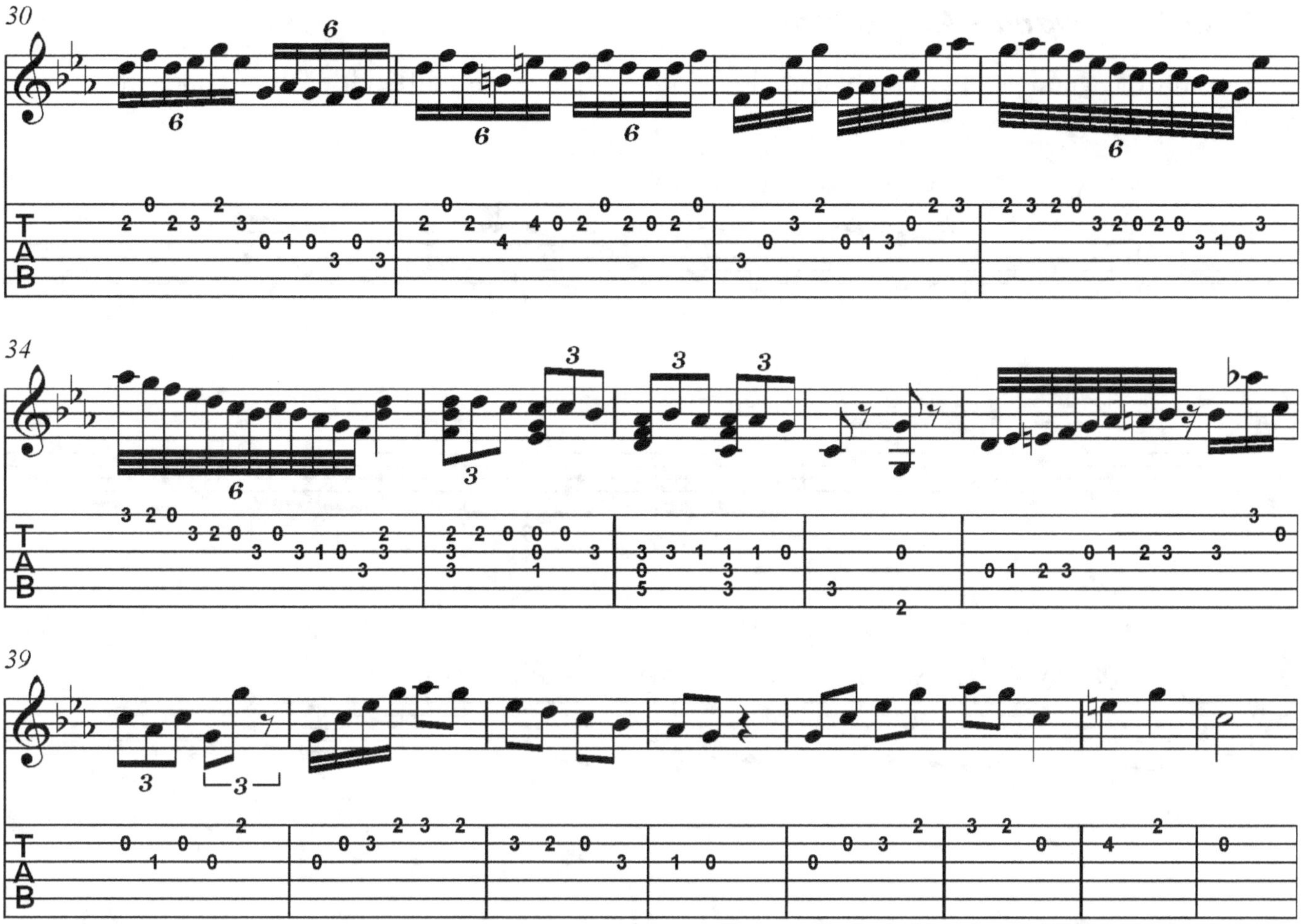

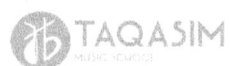

Triplet *Nahawand* – A. Mukhtar

This exercise is good practice combining high *risha* technique with difficult positions and extensive use of arpeggios.

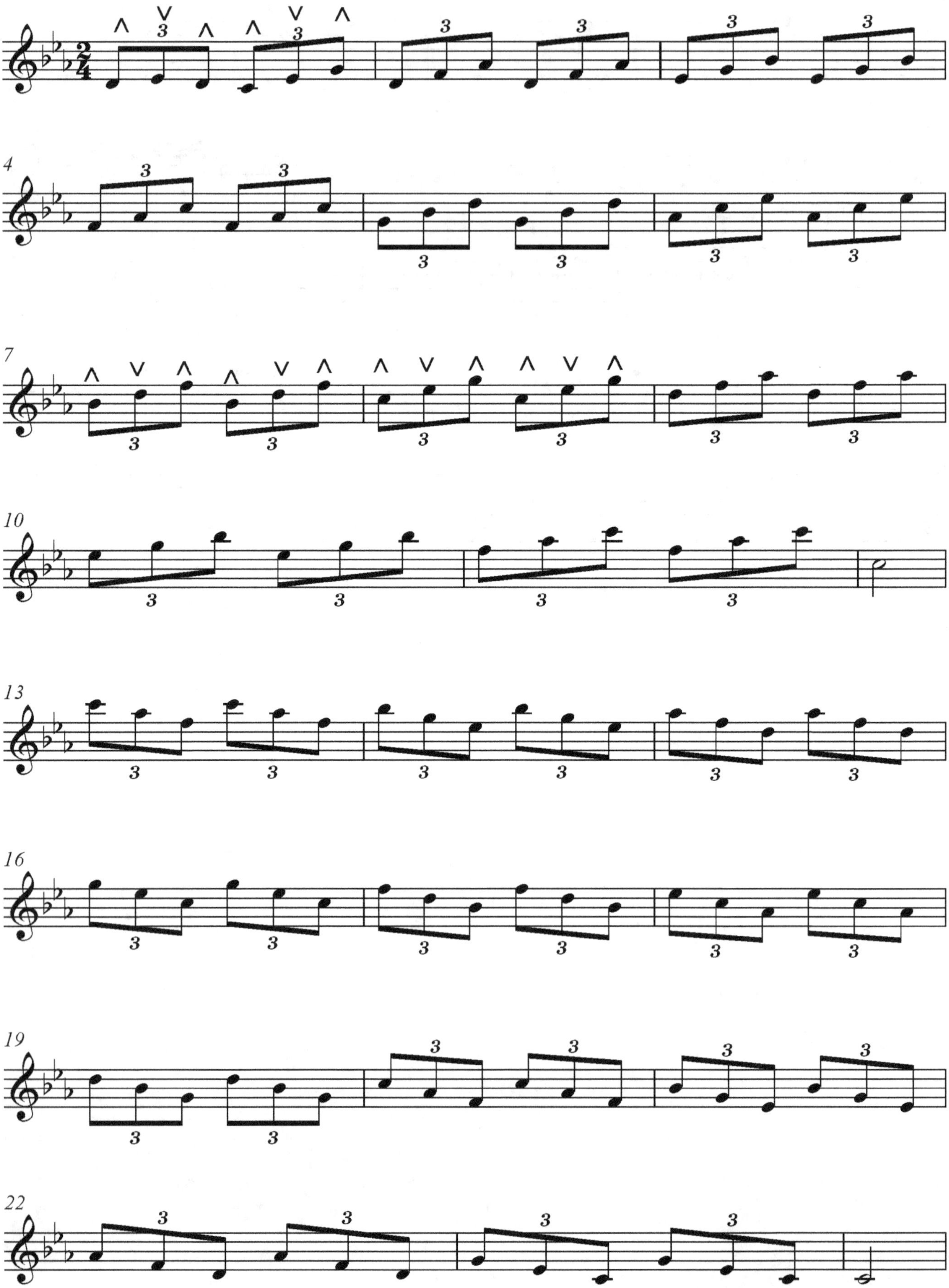

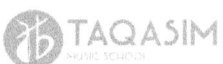

41

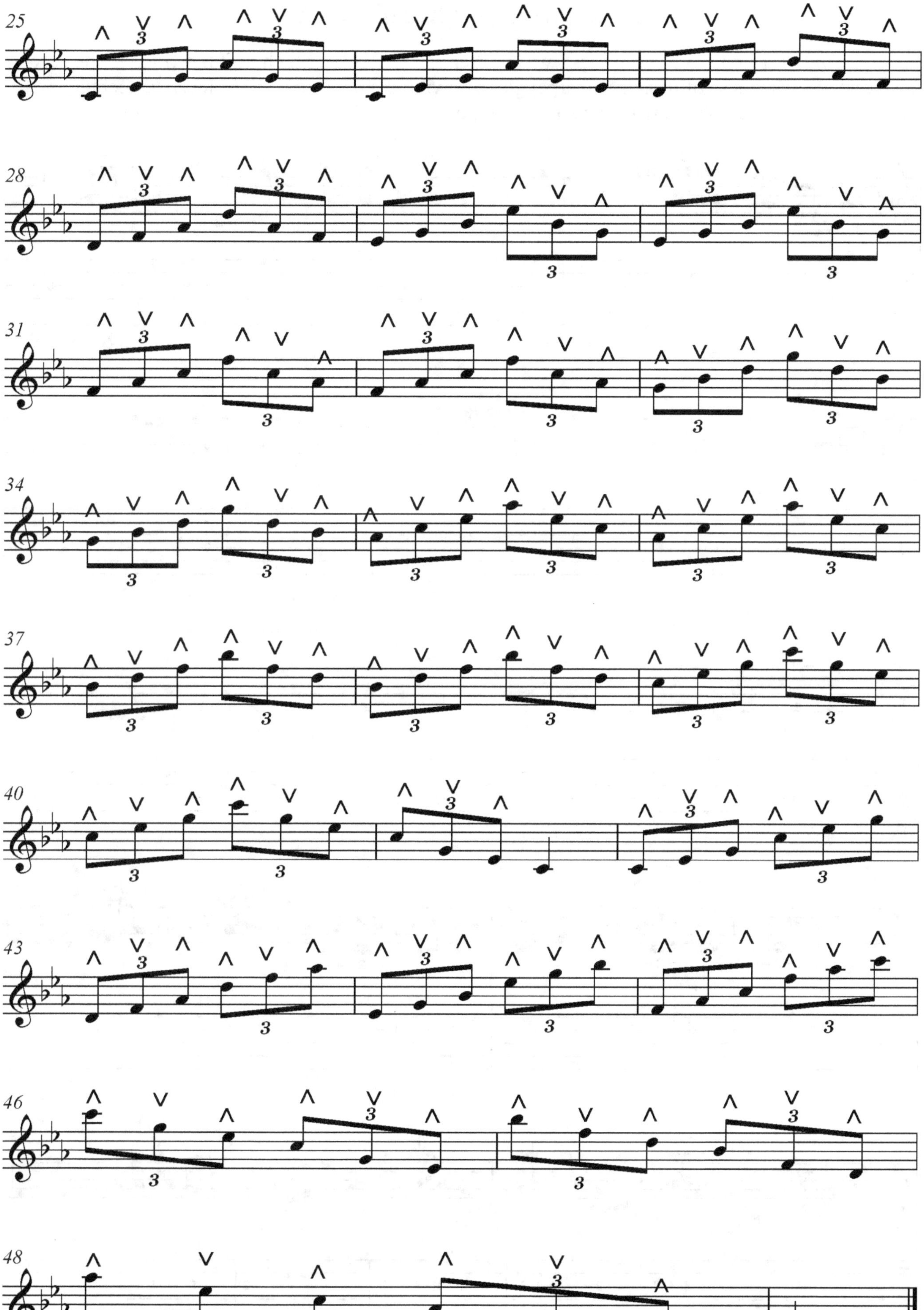

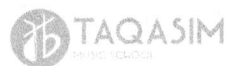

Leyta Li Jinaah – Sharif M. Haider

Leyta Li Jinaah (I Long to Have Wings), was written in the 1940's. Much of it is written in the second octave. It also uses a lot of triplets and arpeggios allowing the player to use triplet *risha* techniques. The goal of this piece is to play it using a fast tempo.

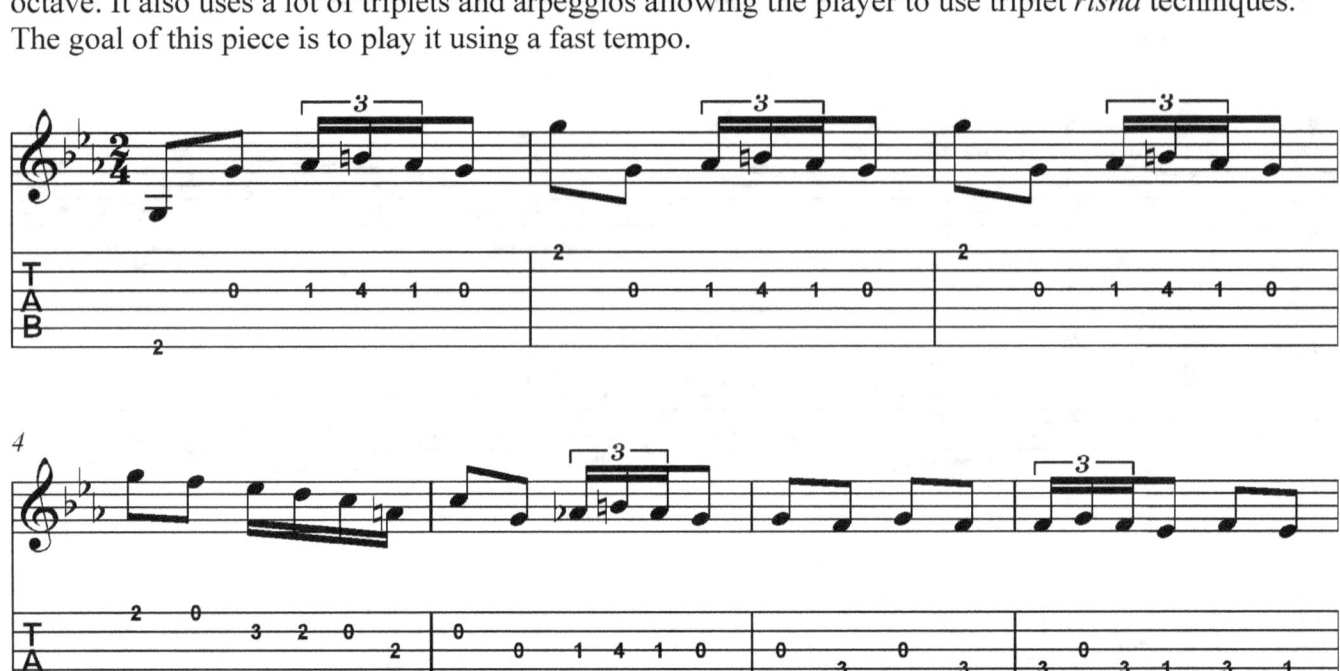

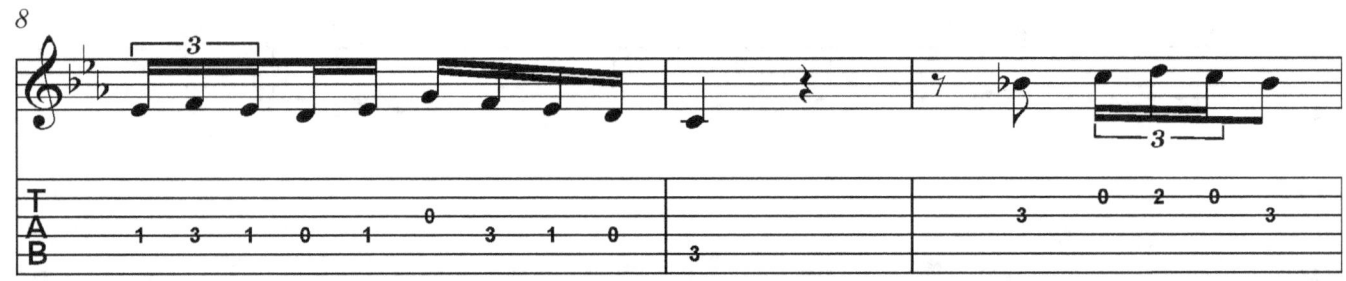

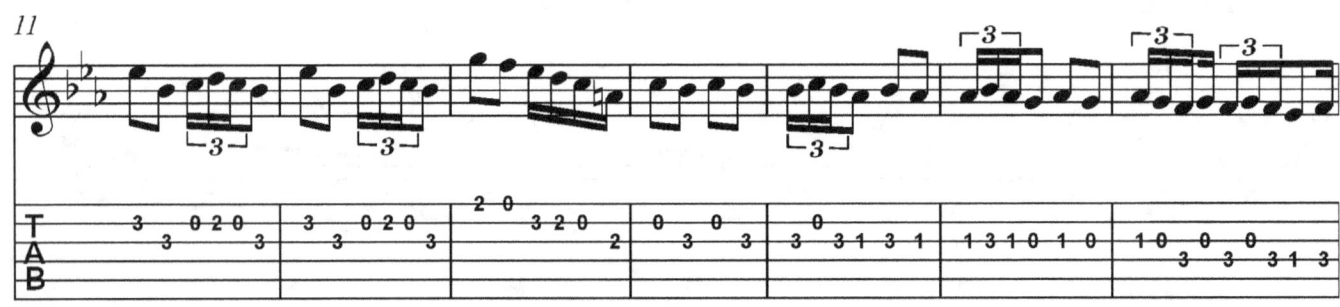

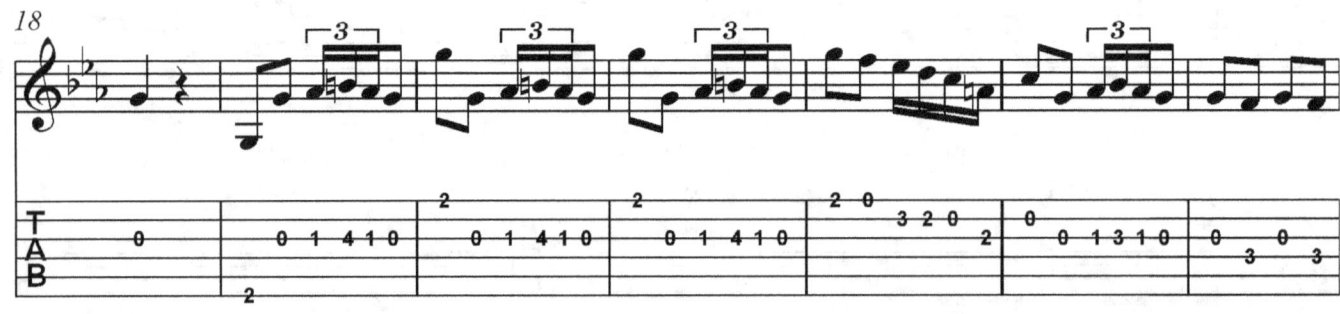

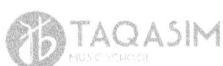

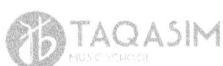

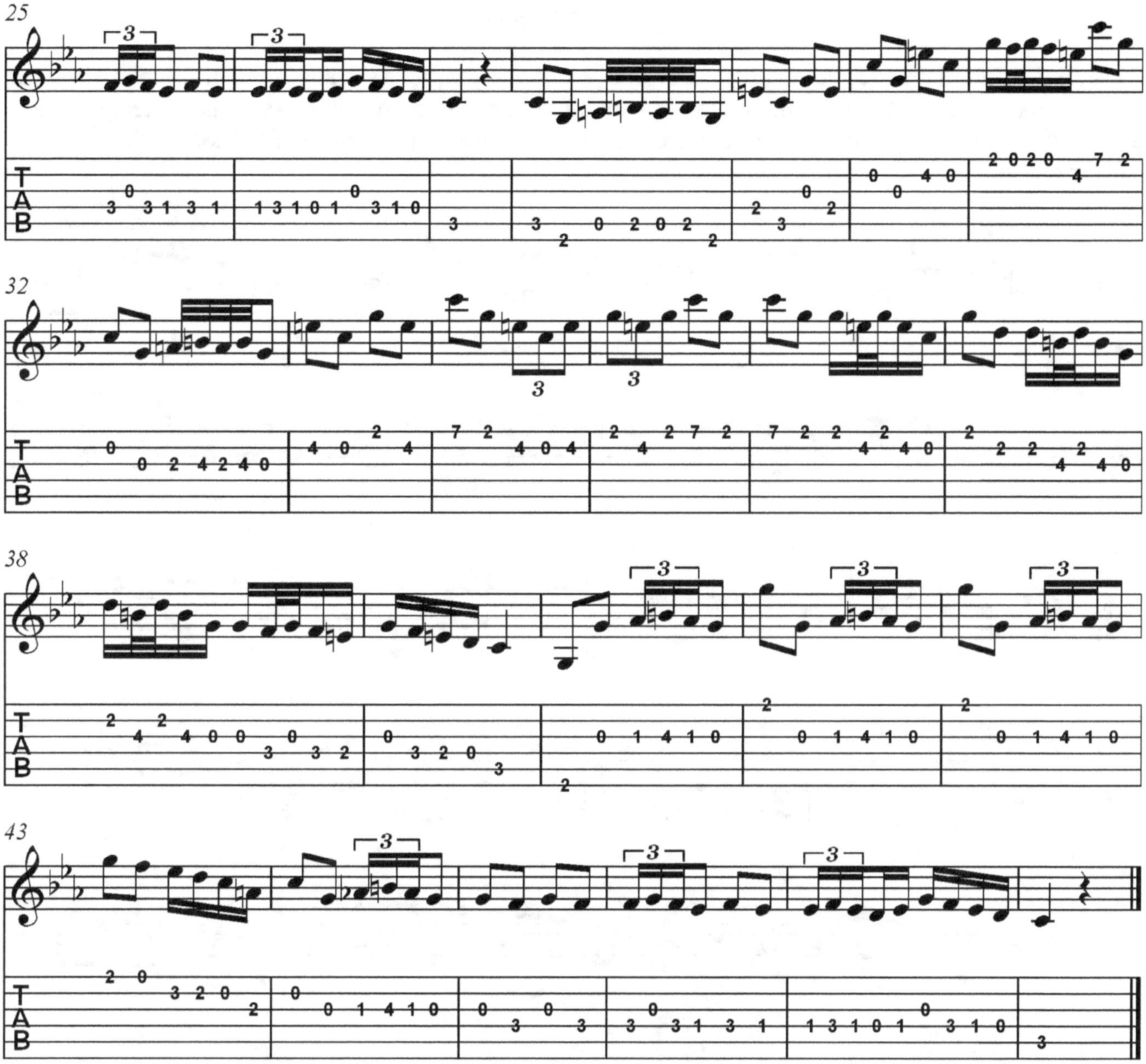

43

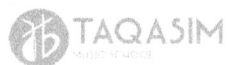

Etude – **Mukhtar**

This *etude* is good practice combining *qarar* and *jawab* with triplet risha strokes. This combination can be seen in bars 12 to 16. The combination in bars 29 to 32 are written using a syncopated tempo. Begin at a slow tempo before picking up the pace playing it as fast as possible without losing the tempo or tonal precision.

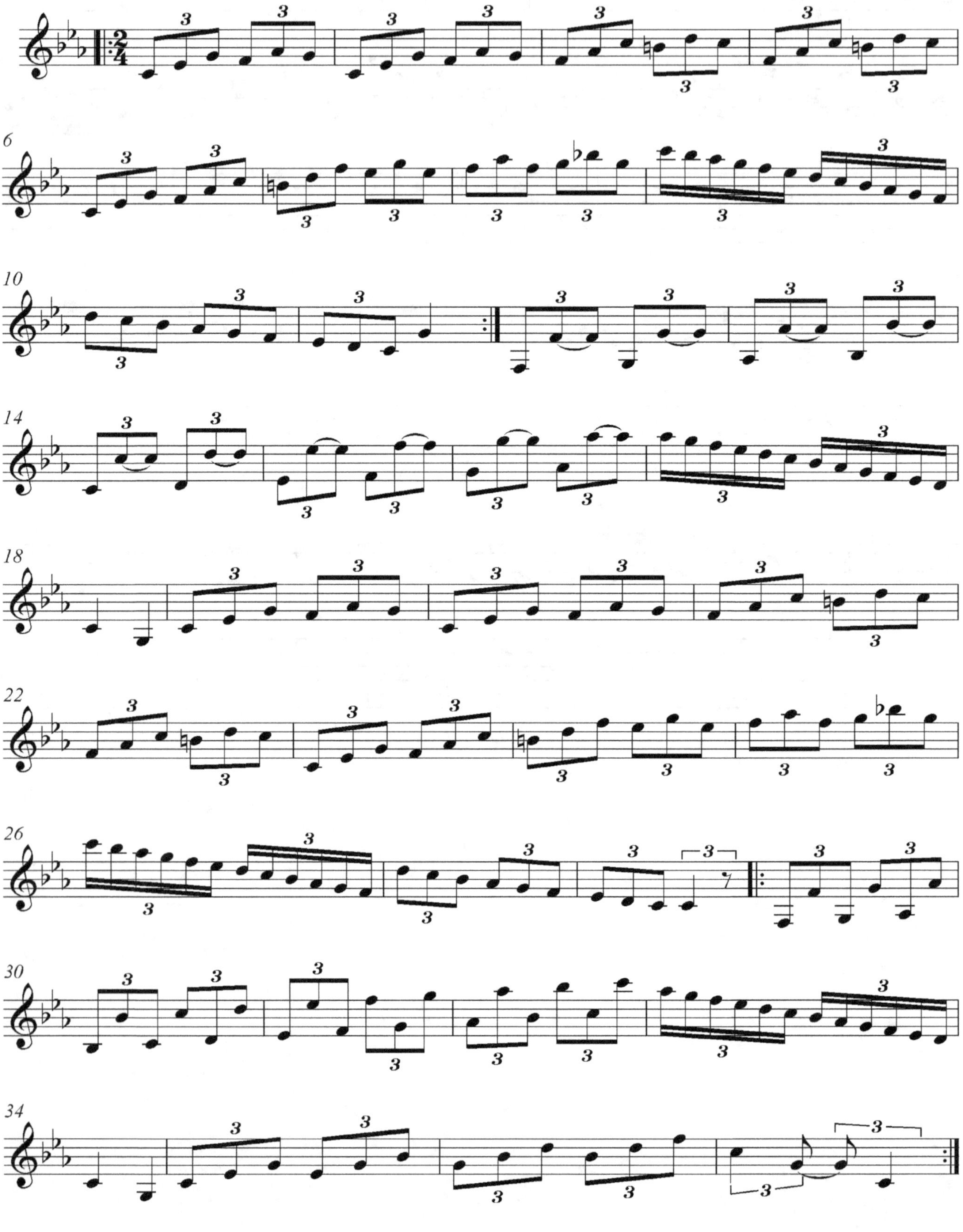

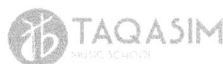

Childhood *Ajam* Fa – Ahmed Mukhtar

This piece is written by Ahmed Mukhtar, on *Ajam* Fa played at a slow tempo. It uses doubled notes, chromatic scales and is good practice for the 3rd octave of *Ajam* Fa as well as *qarar* and *jawab*. Use the thumb of your right hand to play the open Fa string (Fa *qarar* – first string).

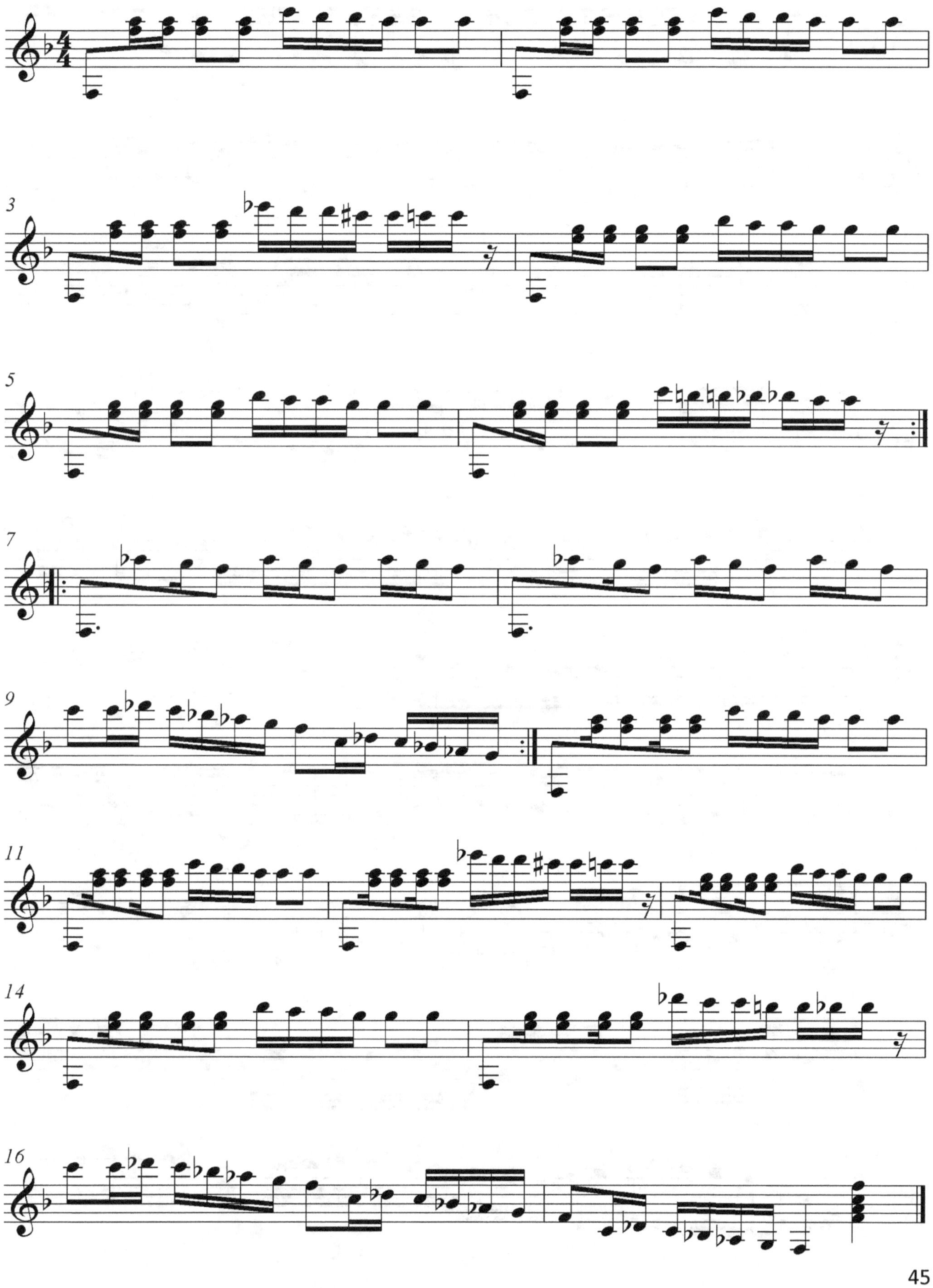

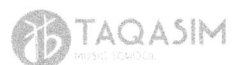

Al-Tel w al-Qamar (Samaa'i Ajam Fa) – Khalid M. Ali

This piece, *Al-Tel w al-Qamar* (The Hill & the Moon) was written by Khalid Mohammad Ali in 1992.

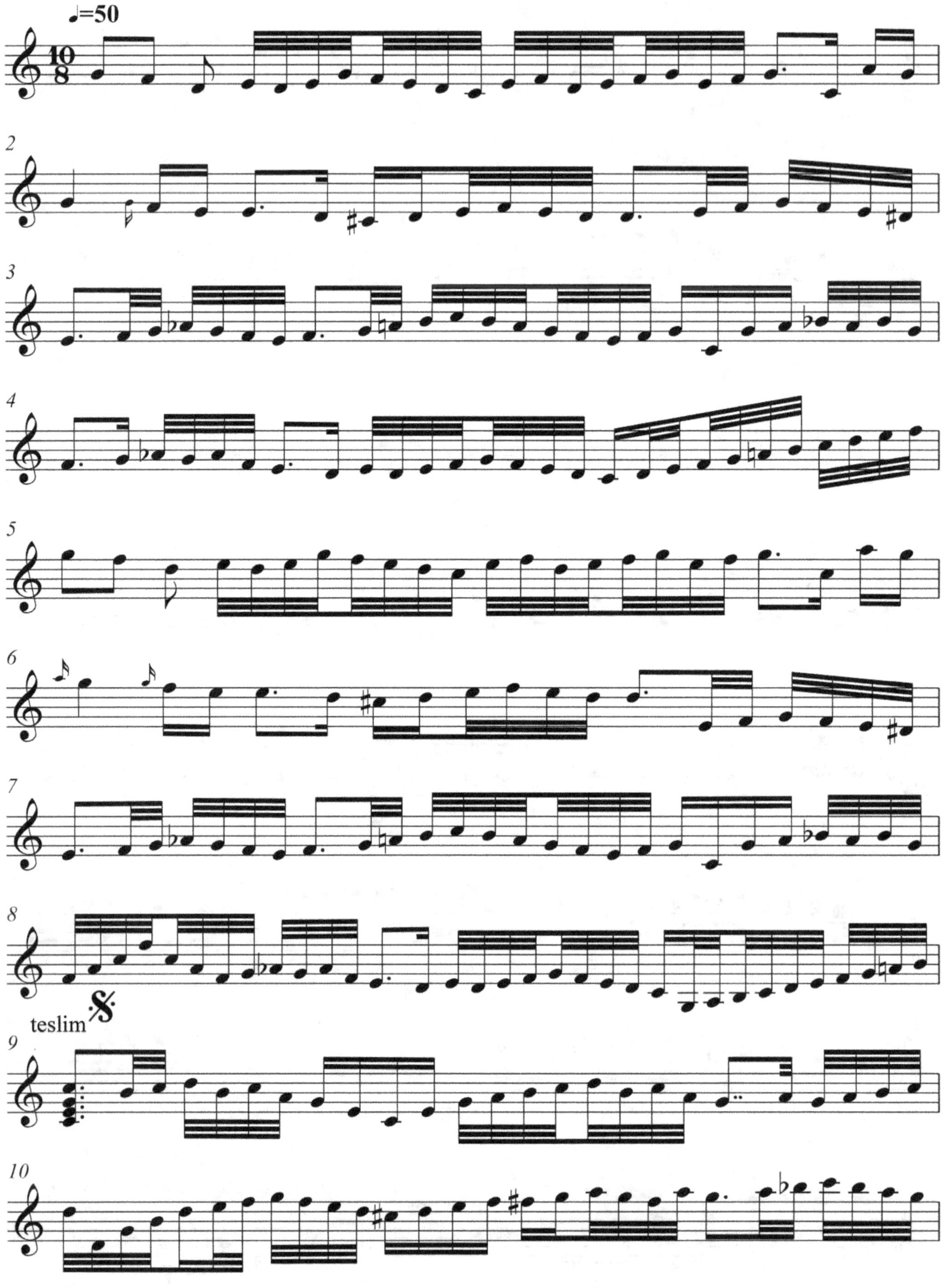

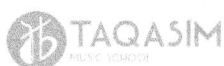

11

12 FIN

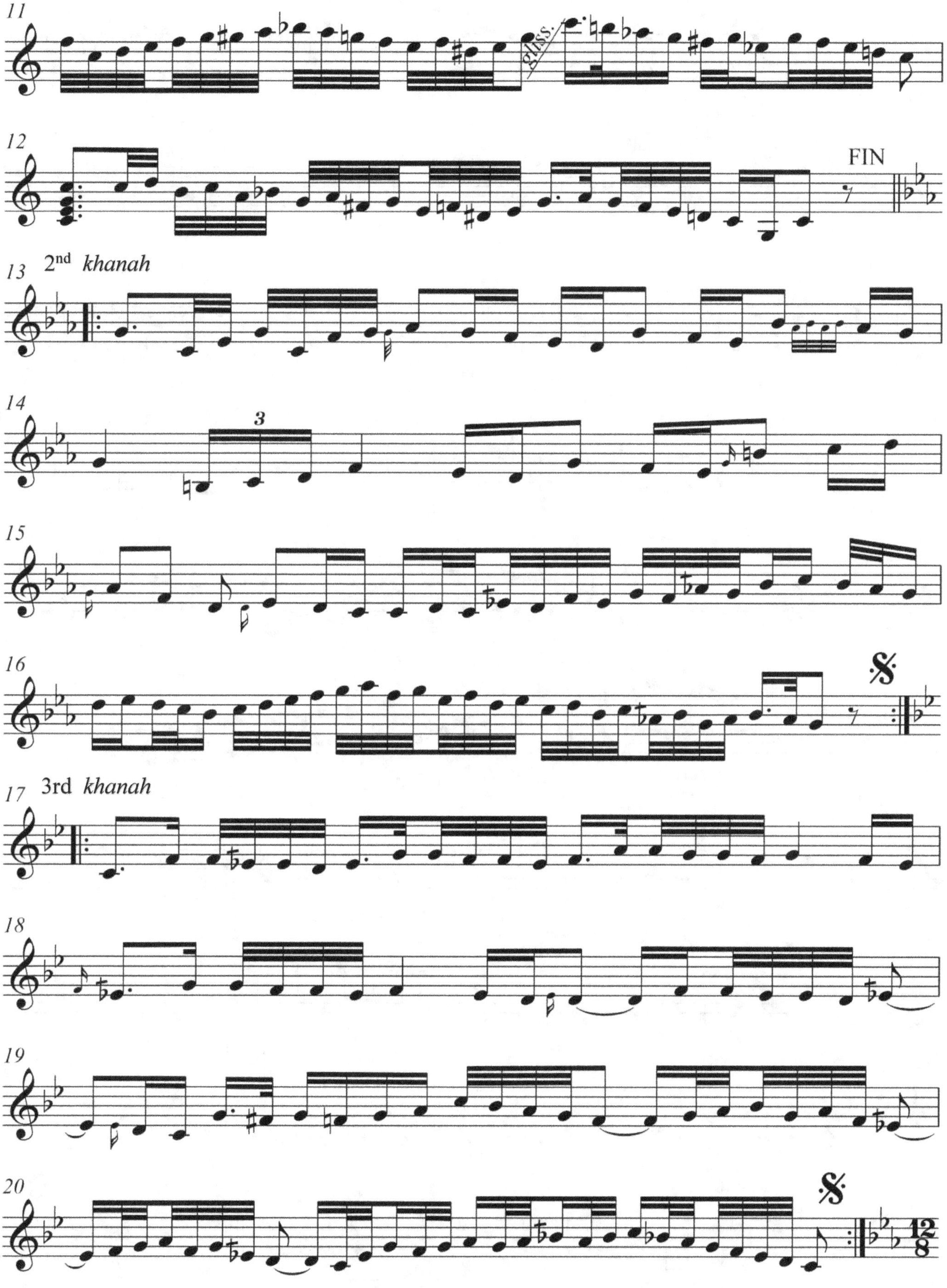

13 2nd *khanah*

14

15

16

17 3rd *khanah*

18

19

20

47

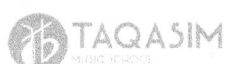

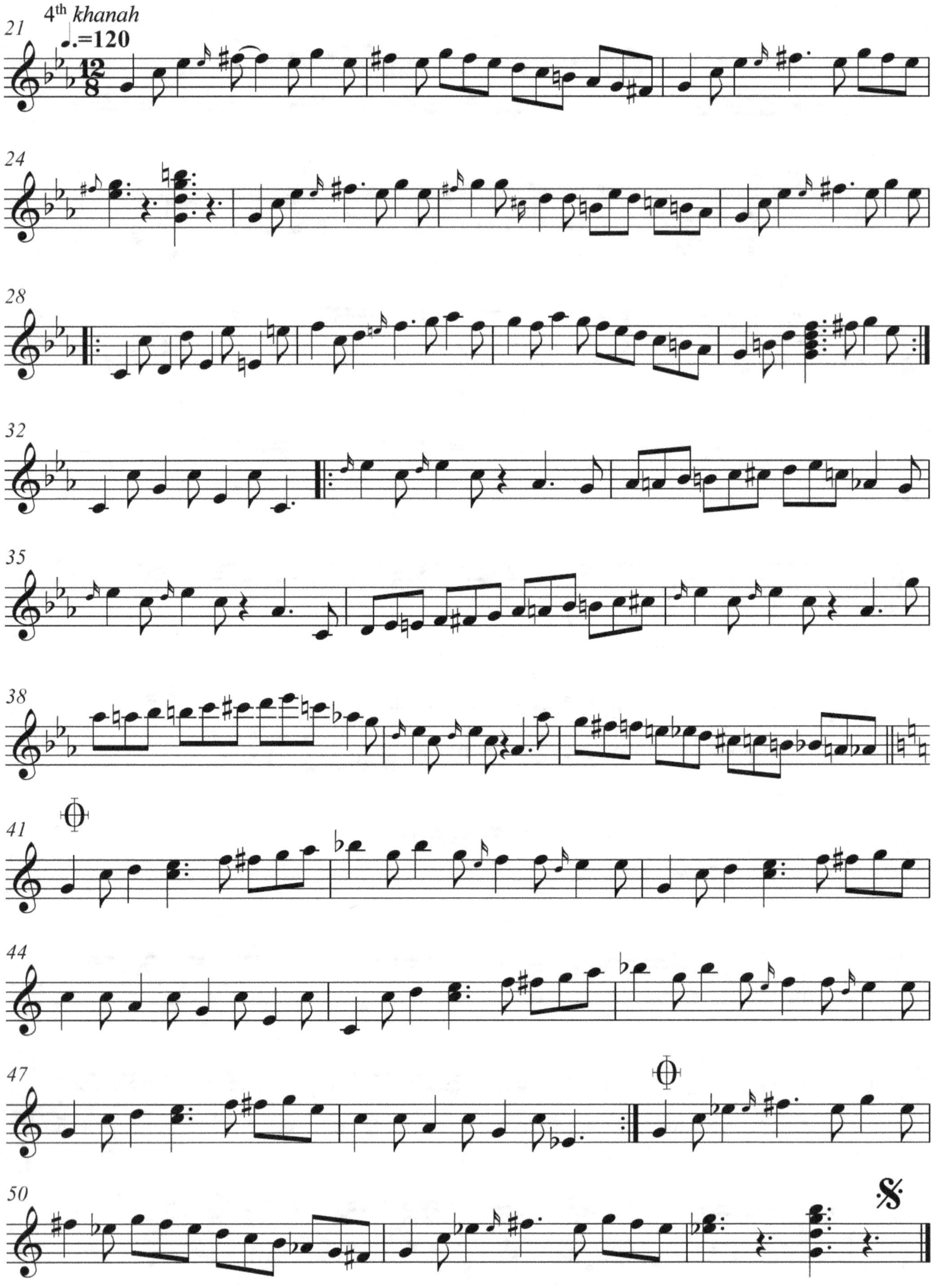

4th *khanah*

$\bullet. = 120$

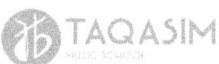

Maqam Hijaz – Trills on One String

The scores below illustrate the correct finger patterns to practice *trills* on one string in the 1st, 2nd and 3rd positions for *Maqam Hijaz* La, Re, Sol and Do. After practicing the pattern at a slow pace using precise finger placement and tones, begin to speed up the tempo without losing tonal precision.

Trill Exercise – *Hijaz* La (2nd string)

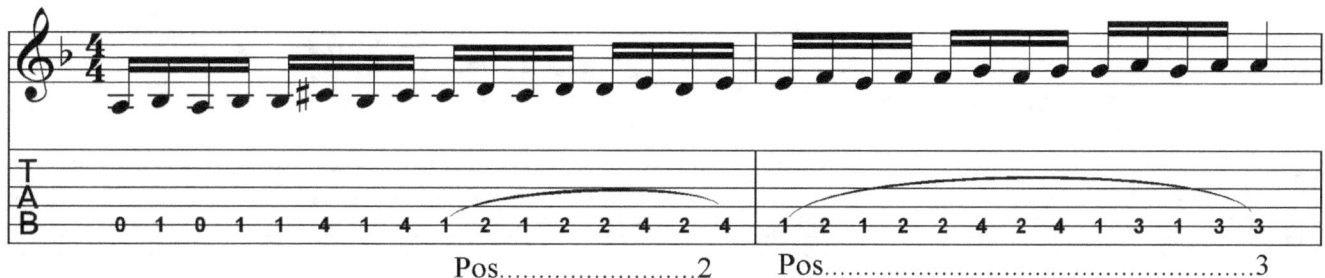

Trill Exercise – *Hijaz* Re (3rd string)

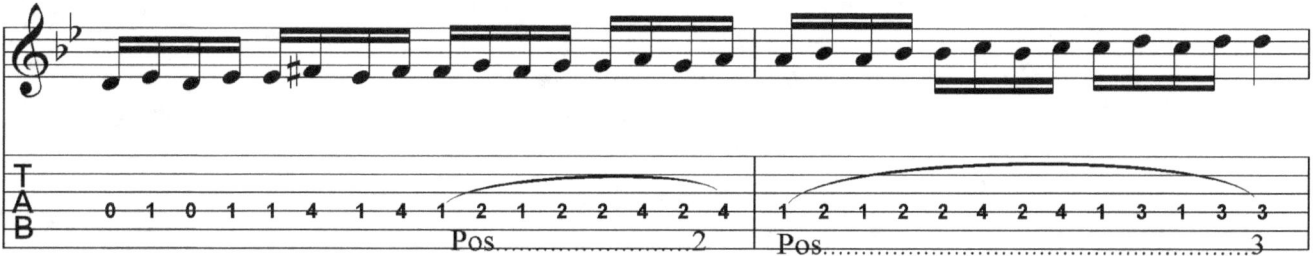

Trill Exercise – *Hijaz* Sol (4th string)

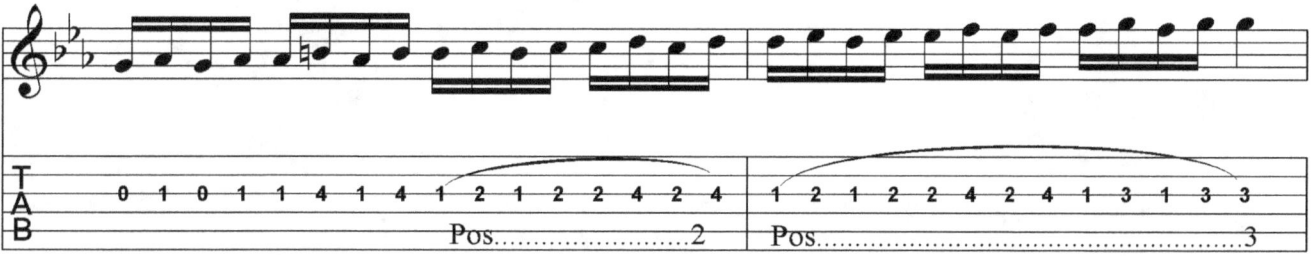

Trill Exercise – *Hijaz* Do (5th string)

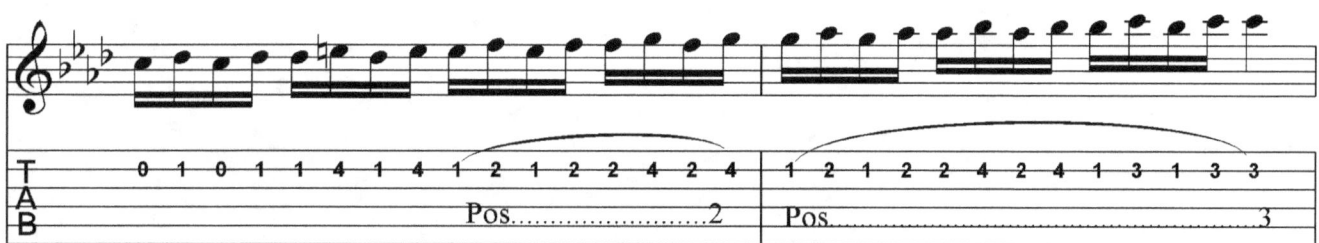

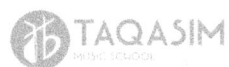

Maqam Tarzanween

Maqam Taqrzanween is a secondary *maqam* from the *Kurd* family. It is a *maqam* that is rarely used nowadays.

Tarzanween Fa

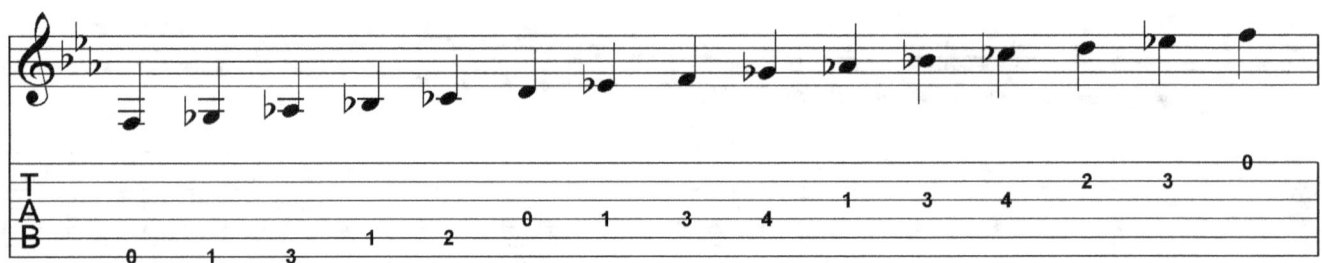

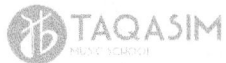

Samaa'i Hijaz Do – Ahmed Mukhtar

This piece, also titled *Samaa'i Ghiyaab,* was composed using 3 octaves of Maqam Hijaz Do. It is a complex piece that uses multiple *maqamaat* and if transposed, will allow the learner to practice high levels of technique.

Maqam Tarzanween is used in the 3rd *khanah* in bar 11.

If the oud being used to play is tuned Do to do (Do, Sol, La, Re, Sol, Do), this piece can be to *Hijaz* Sol. Transposing the piece will help strengthen and progress finger and *risha* techniques while covering new positions on the oud.

The piece can be viewed on YouTube.

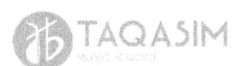

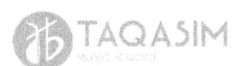

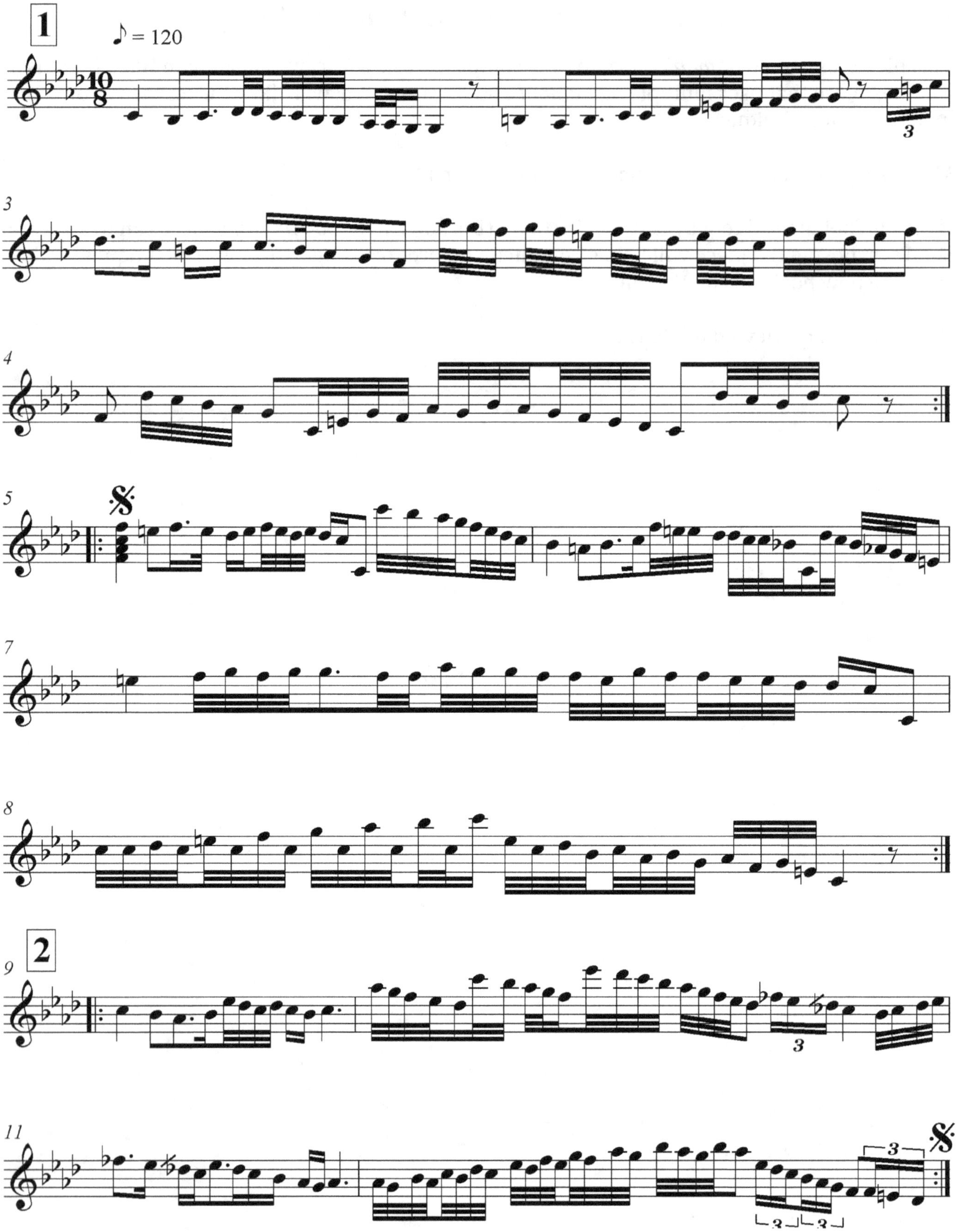

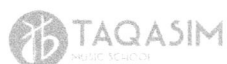

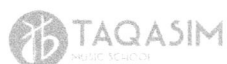

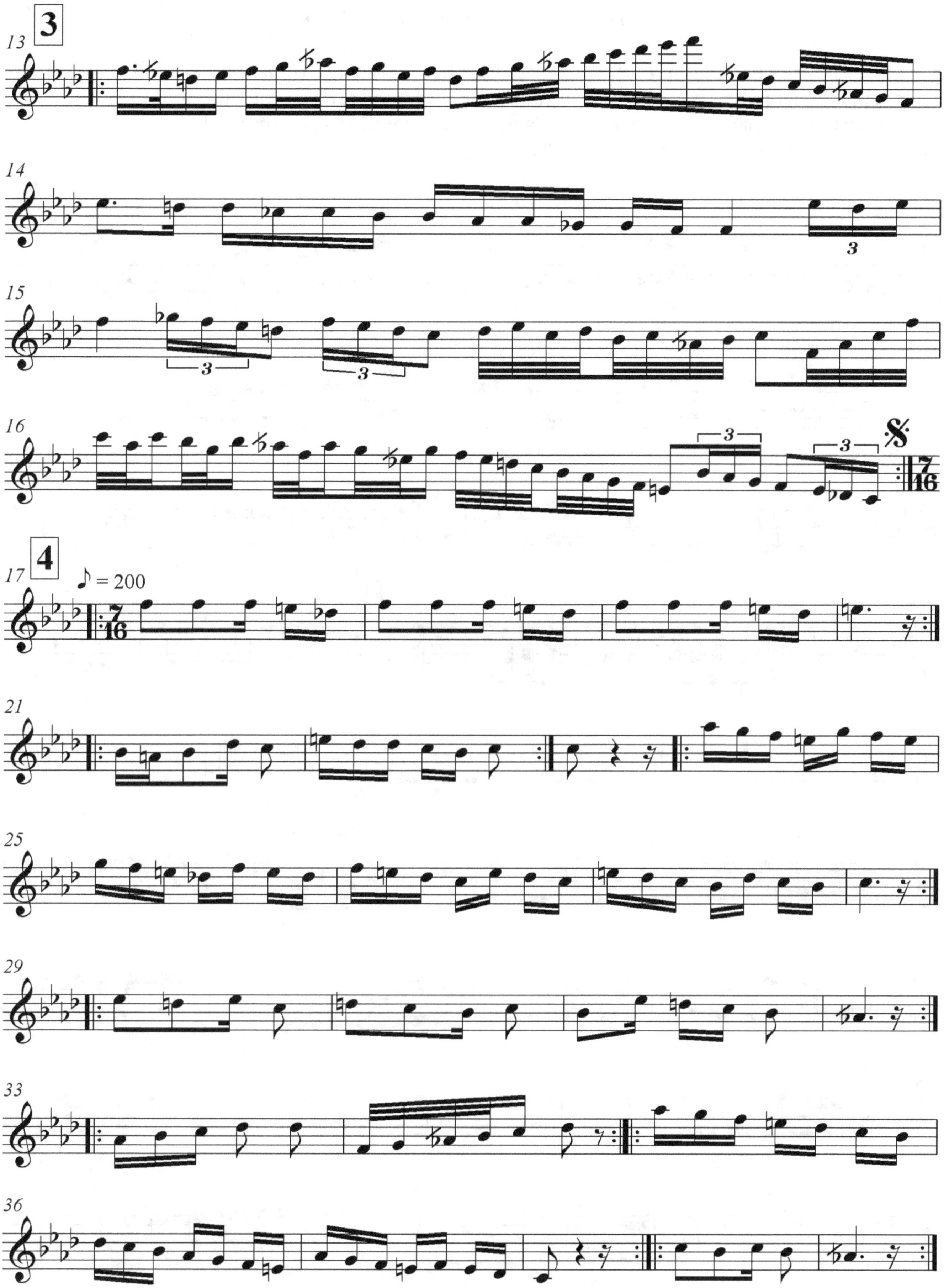

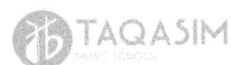

Aspania – **Ahmed Mukhtar**

Aspania is written in *Maqam Hijaz Kar* Fa, a secondary *maqam* of *Hijaz* that is rarely played from Fa. It is played from the 2nd octave (also called the middle octave on the oud) and the 3rd octave using only the 6th string. Its main rhythm is 6/8. However, this sometimes changes to a 2/8 rhythm. The piece can be viewed on YouTube.

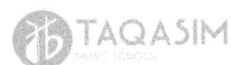

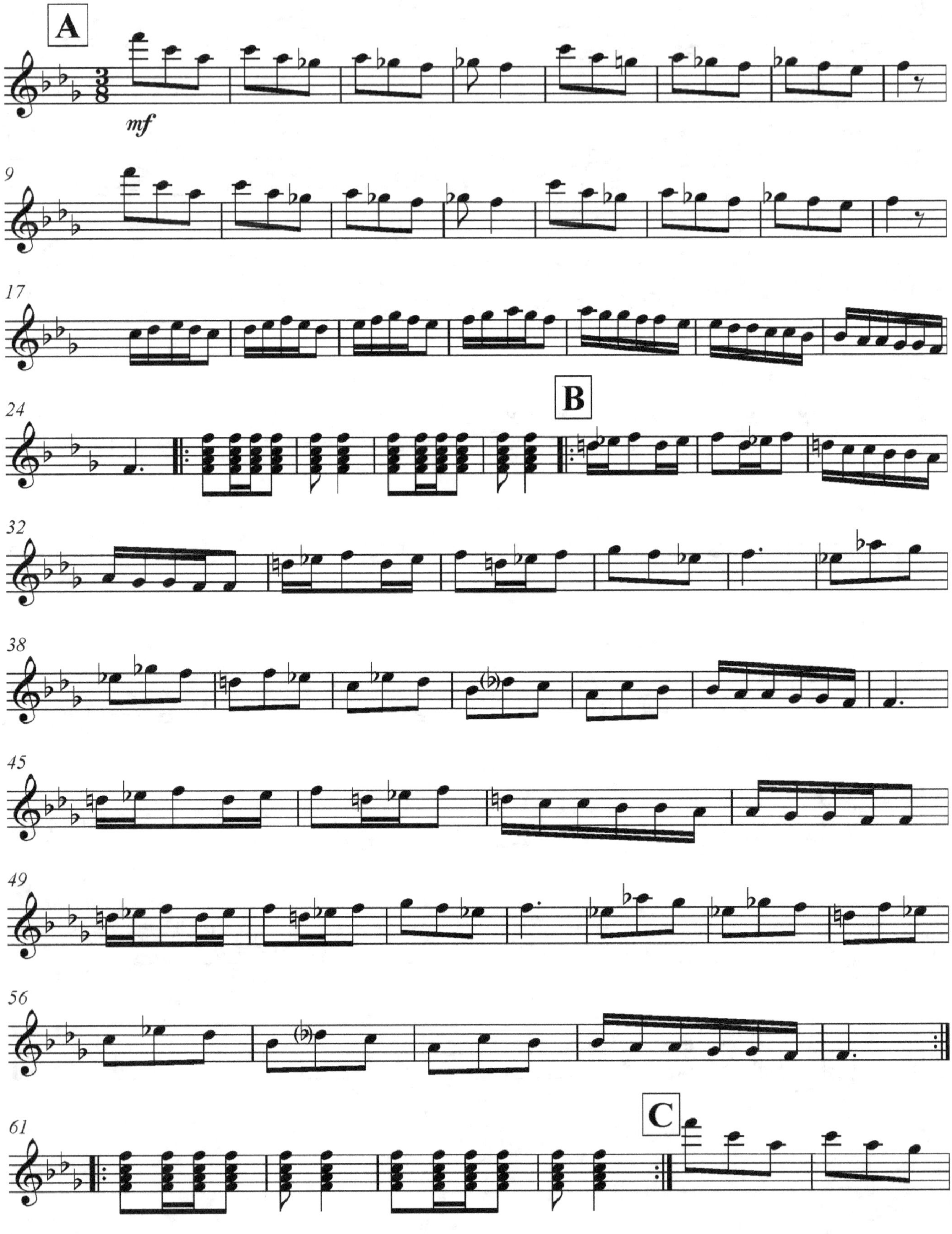

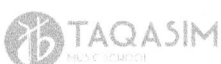

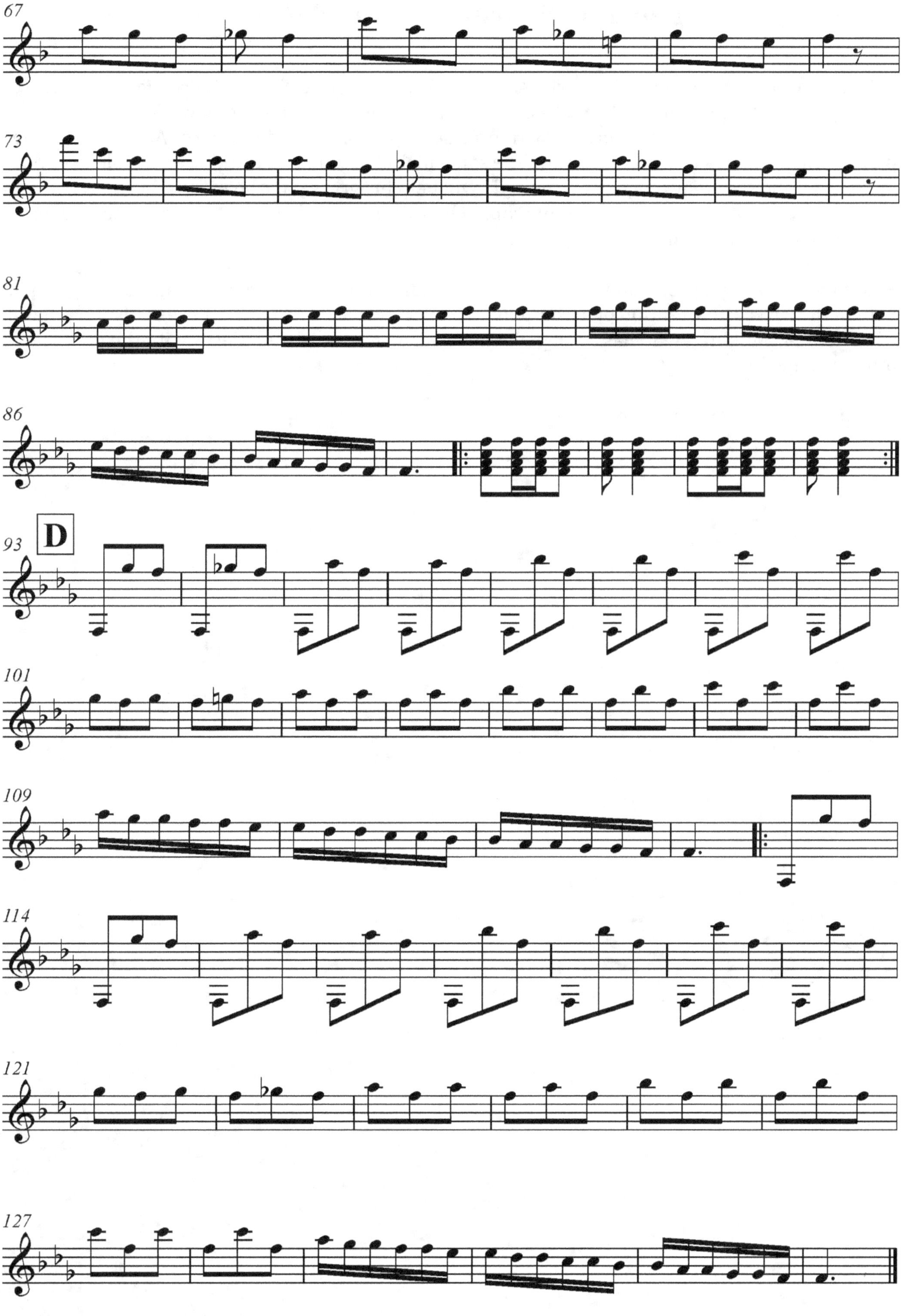

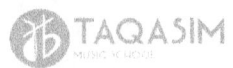

Aspania (with piano) – Ahmed Mukhtar

The style of accompanying the oud with the piano began in the 1950's in Azerbaijan. This style of accompaniment will help you listen to more than one sound and harmony while playing. It also increases your sensitivity to working with precise rhythms. The older style of Arabic ensembles play in unison, i.e. each instrument plays the same melody. While, this kind of ensemble uses both polyphony and harmony. Playing in this style will help progress your hearing to begin to listen to more than one sound while being accompanied by a different instrument. You are encouraged to play in this style to continue to progress this skill.

Studying Western harmony and orchestration in addition to oud composition and playing can help in the successful creation of accompanied pieces such as *Aspenia.* That is exactly what has been done by Mukhtar, who has arranged and performed several oud pieces with the piano and other stringed instruments.

The piece can be viewed on YouTube.

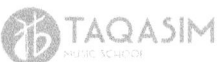

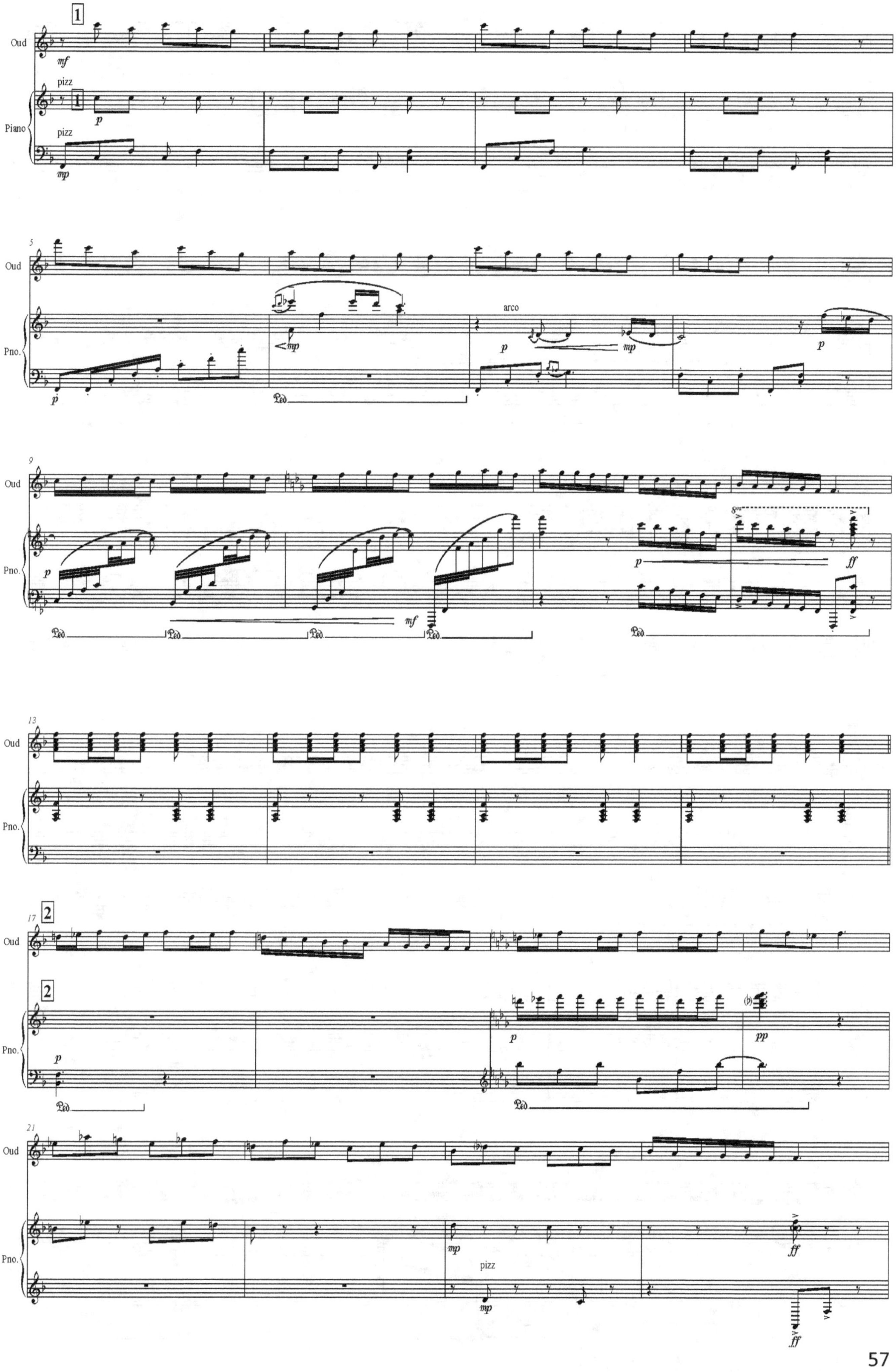

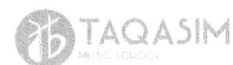

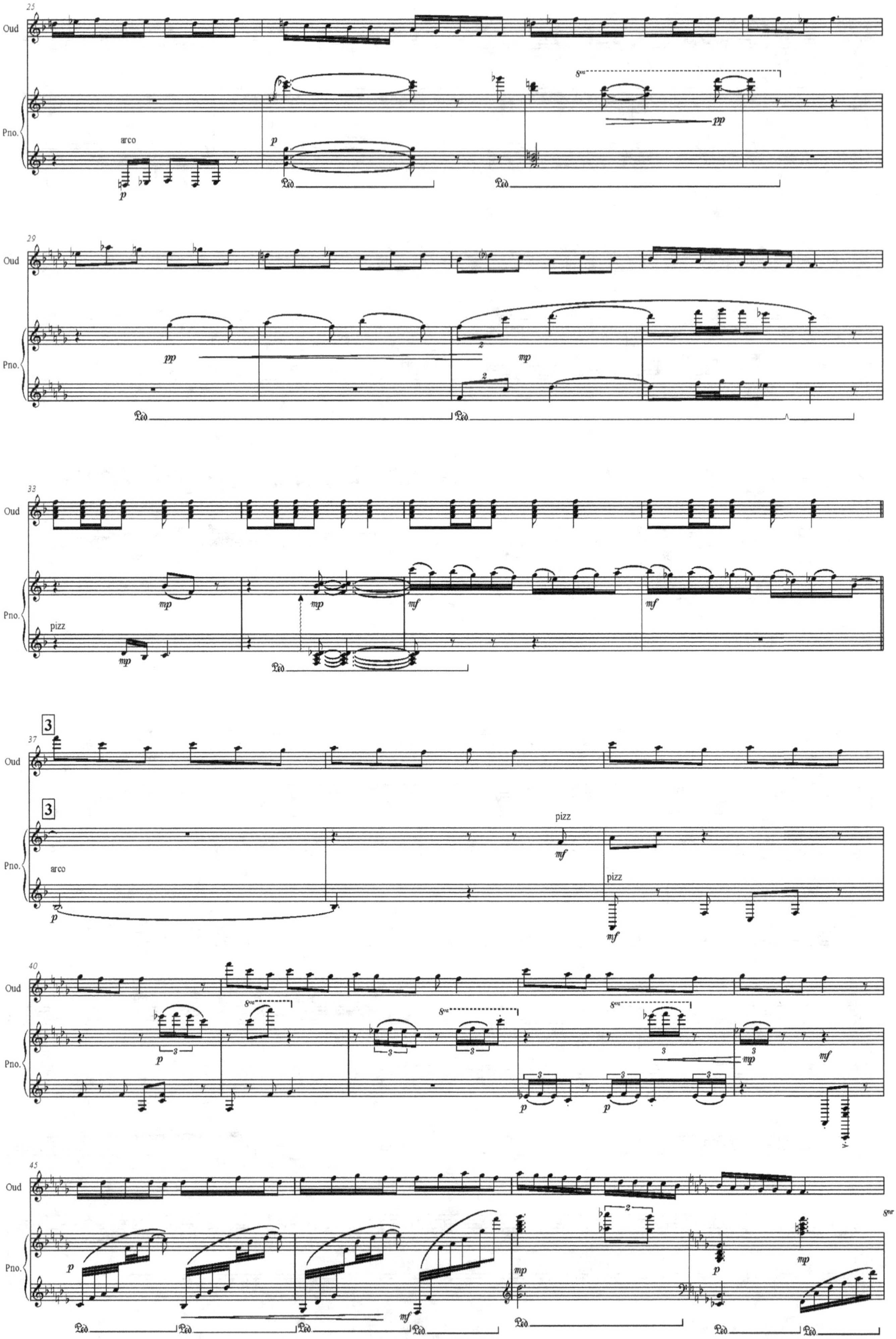

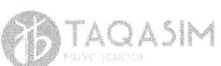

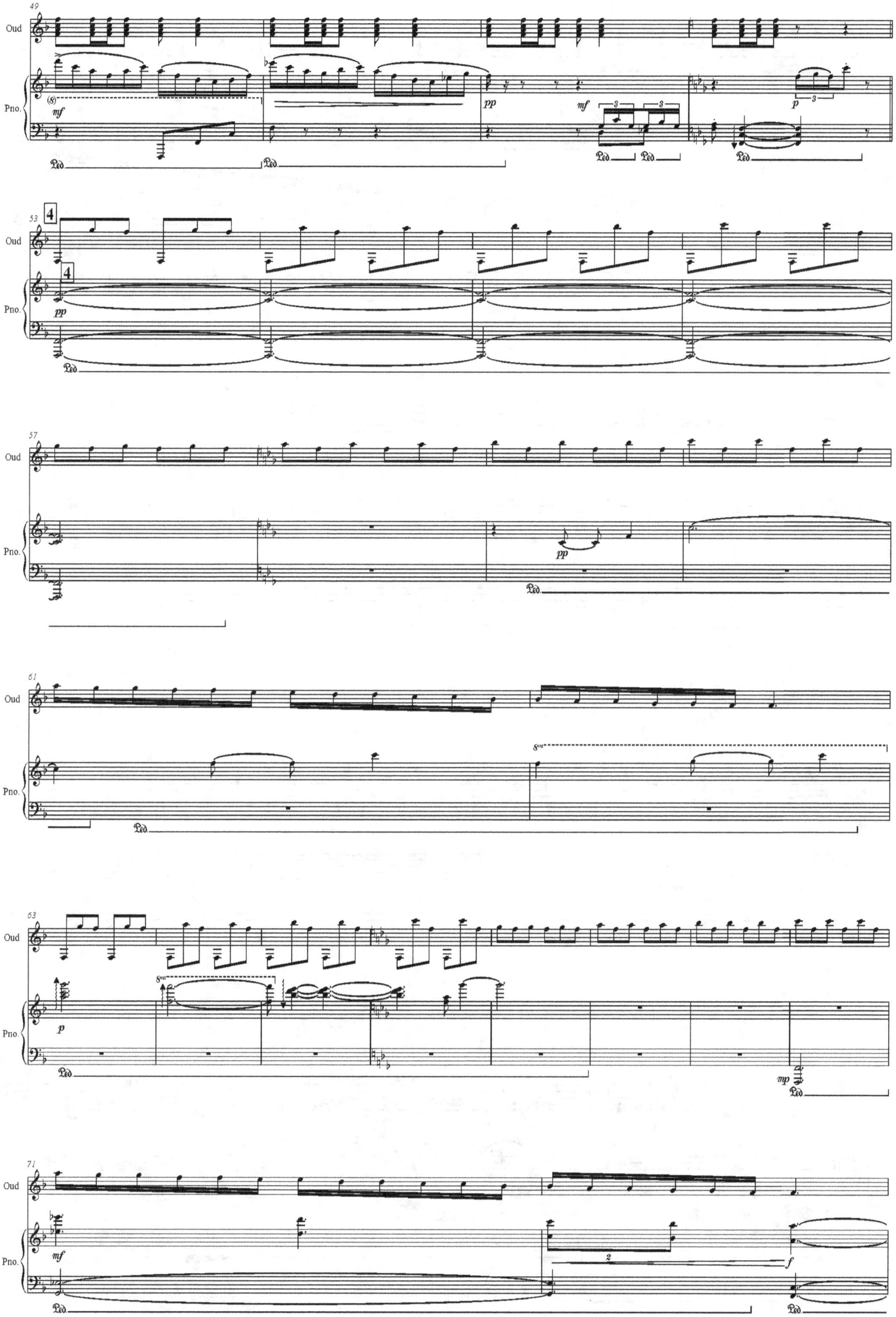

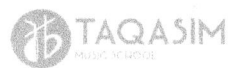

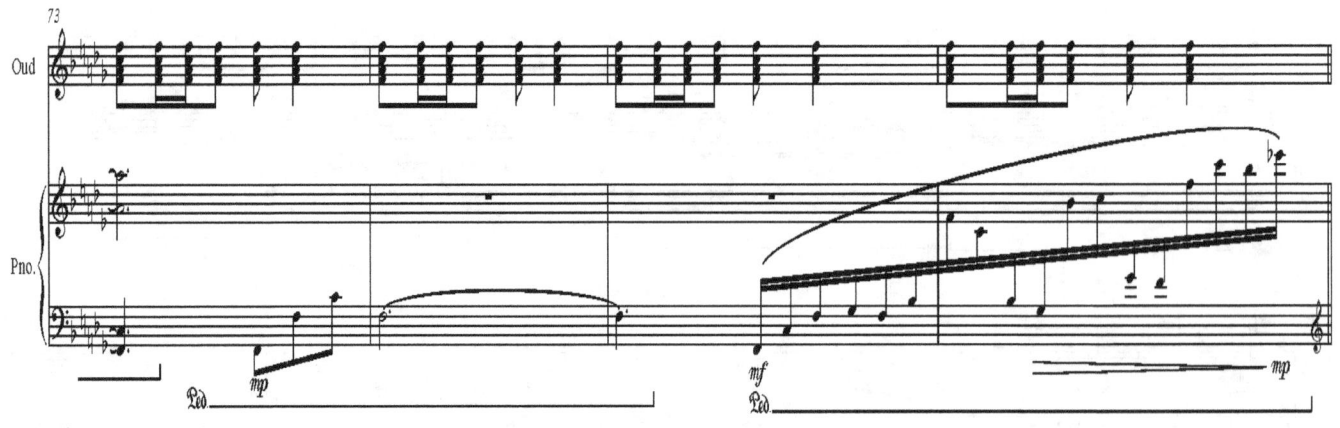

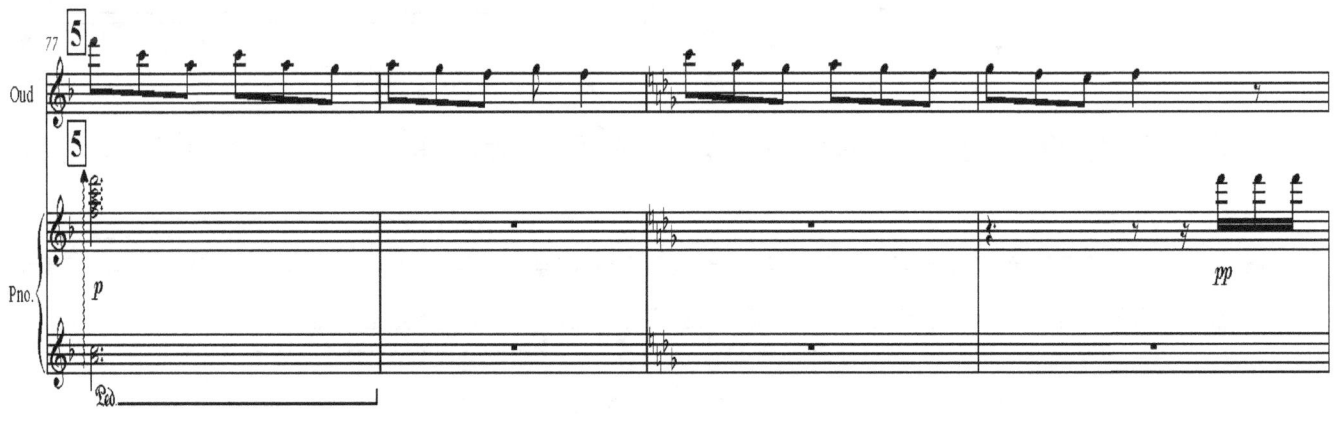

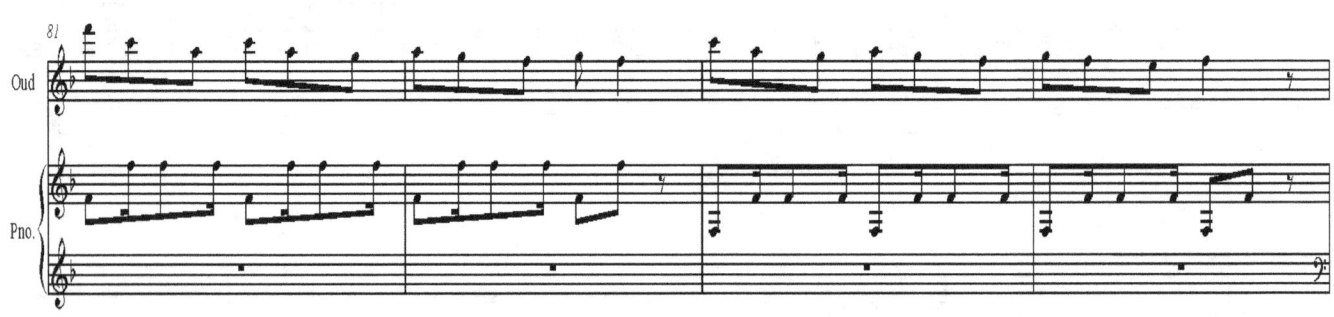

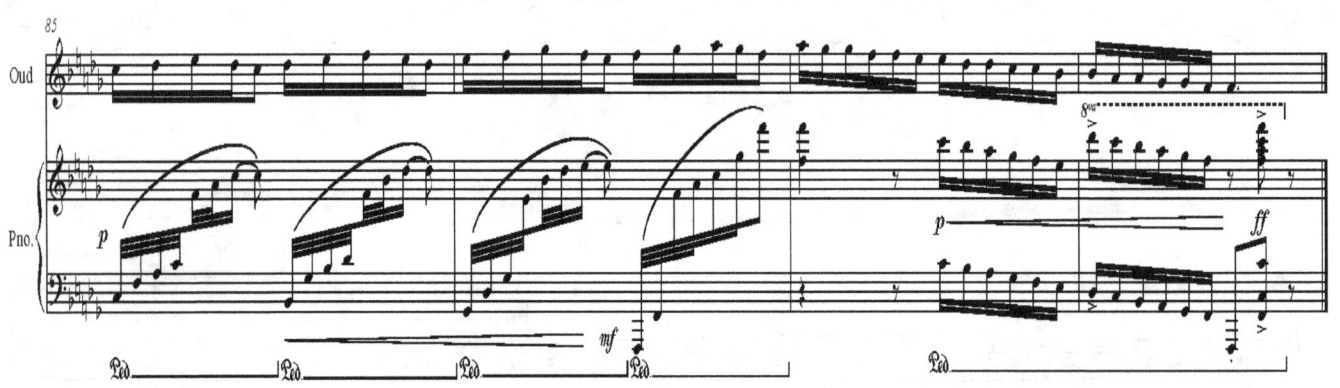

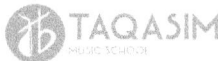

Samaa'i Baghdad (Maqam Kurd) – **Ahmed Mukhtar**

This is the first *samaa'i* that leaves the first 8 bars of music free for the performer to improvise instead of the traditional introduction that is usually written by the composer. This gives the performer more creative opportunity when playing.

Each *khanah* modulates to 2 *maqamaat* rather than just 1 *maqam* in traditional *samaa'is* . For example: the 2nd *khanah* uses both *Ajam* Fa and *Bayat* Sol. The 3rd *khanah* is written using *Hijaz Kar* Re and *Lami*, and the 4th *khanah* uses *Maqam Ajam* Fa and *Kurd* Re. Also, the 4th *khanah* is written using a rhythm that has been created by the composer called *Iqaa'* Mukhtar (Mukhtar Rhythm). It is a combination of 11/16 and 5/8 rhythms.

Many high level techniqies are used when playing this piece such as: playing on the 3rd octave of *Maqam Kurd*; the use of chords; and strummed double notes. A lot of synchopation is used, especially in the 3rd *khanah* when the rhythm changes from 9 beats in bars20 to 11 beats in bar 21.

The piece can be viewed on YouTube.

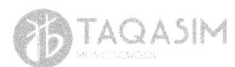

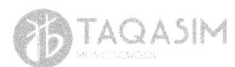

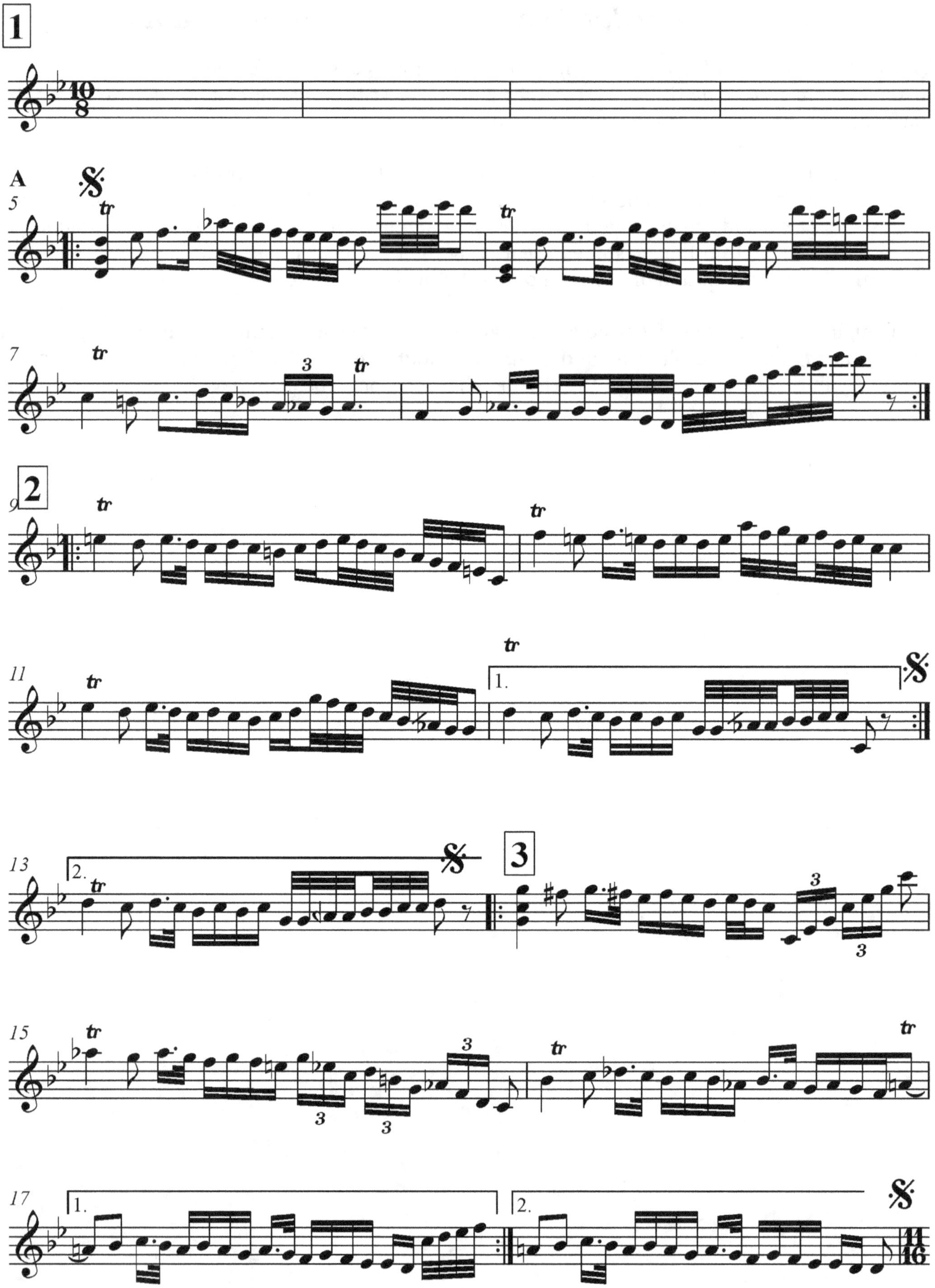

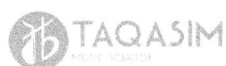

4

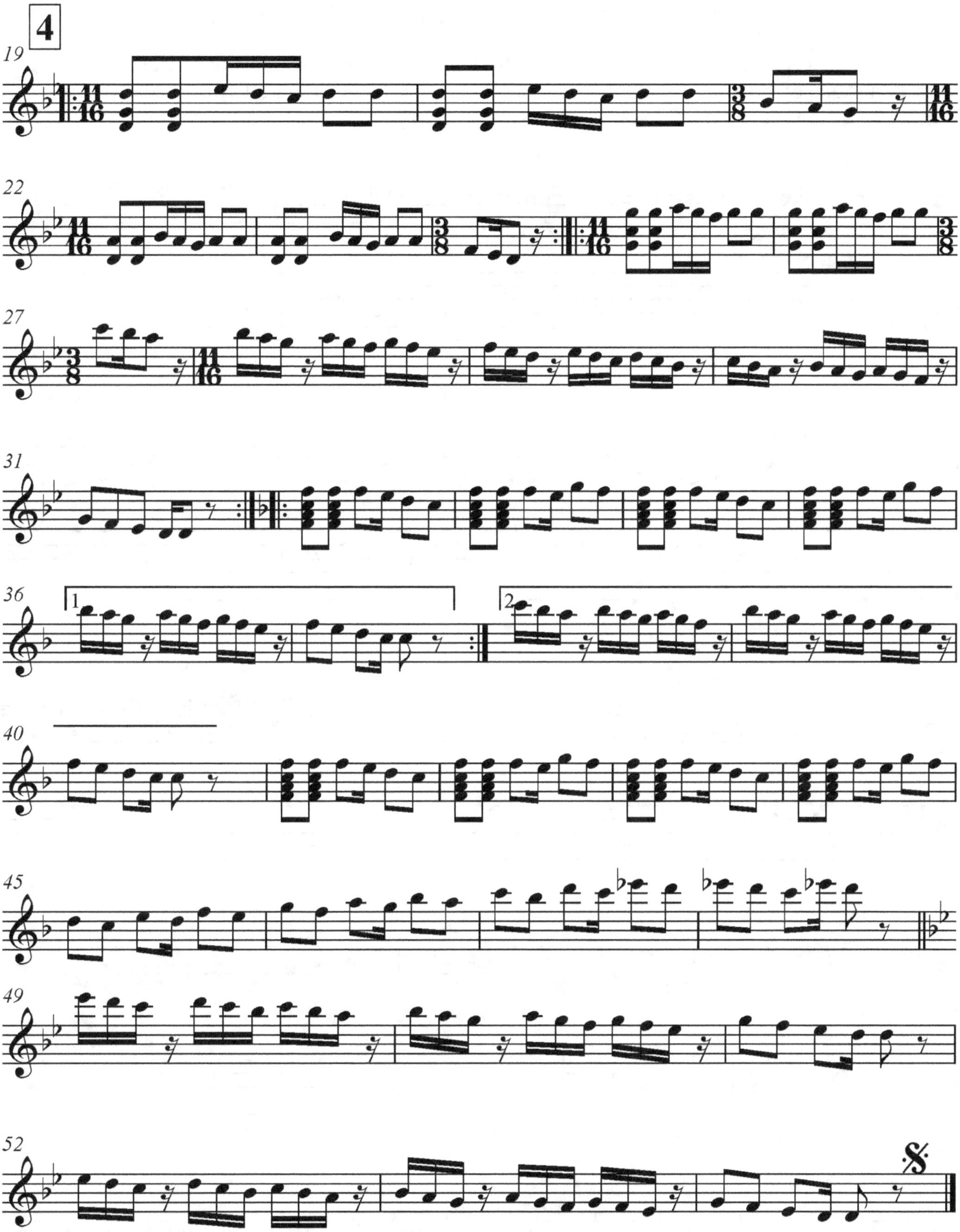

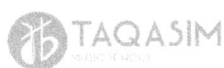

Al-Asfour el-Taa'r (Flying Bird) – Munir Bashir

This is considered to be a master piece because of its use of multiple chromatic notes combined with variations of *Maqam Nahawand Do* using three positions. First, play the piece at a slow tempo, speeding it up at a later stage. Make sure to always maintain tonal precision.

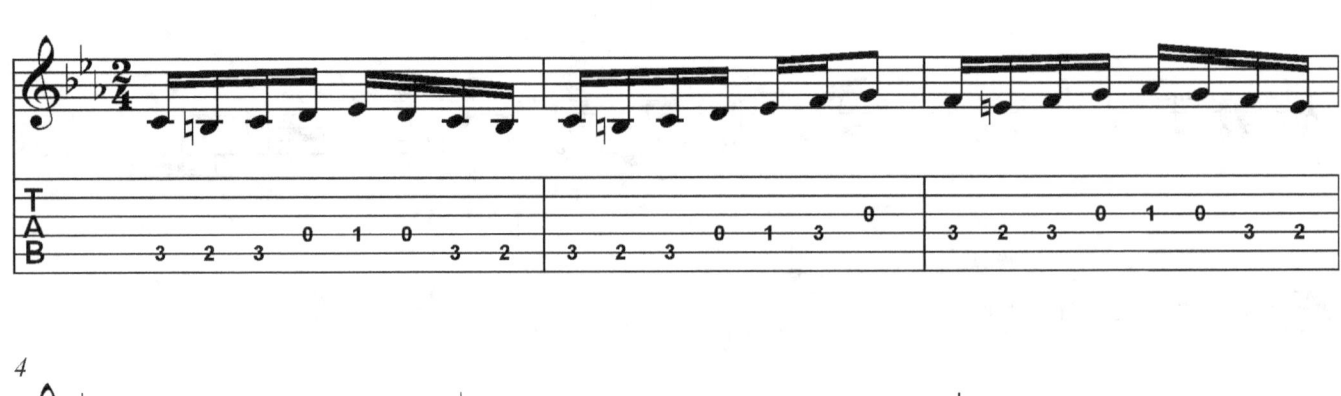

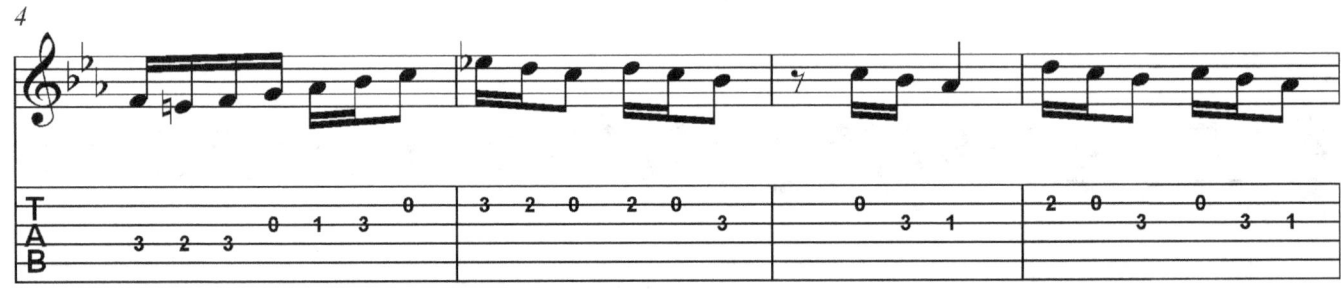

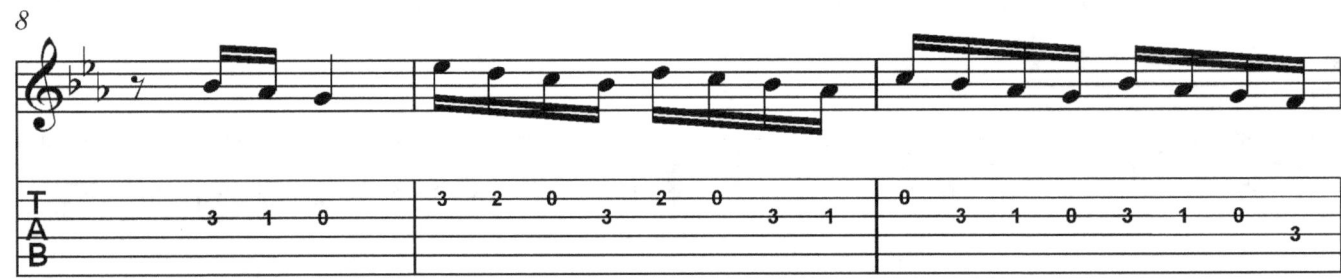

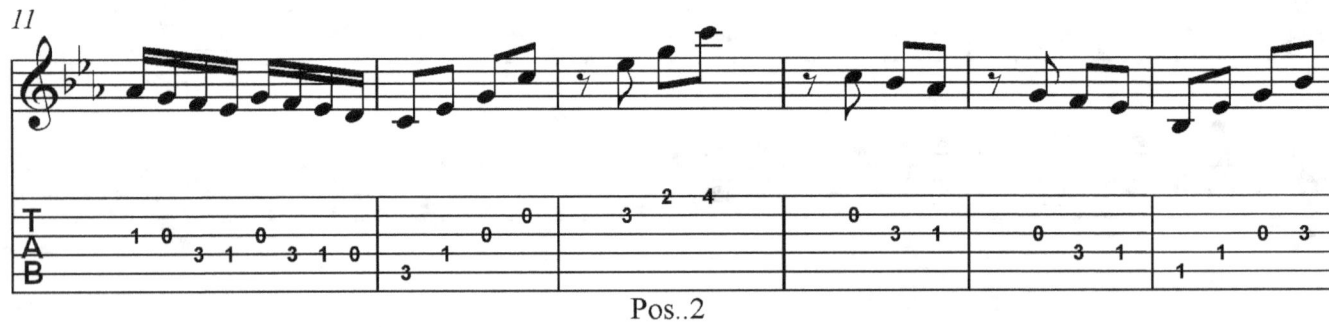

Pos..2

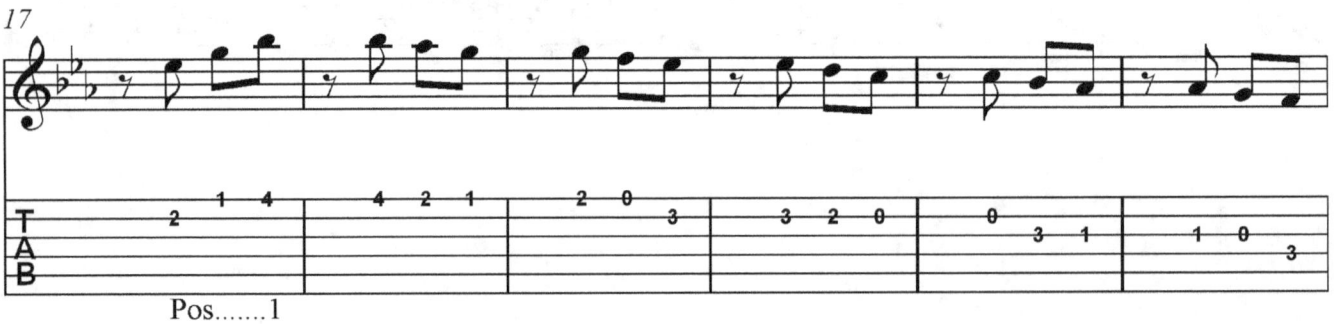

Pos.......1

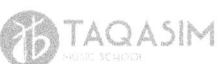

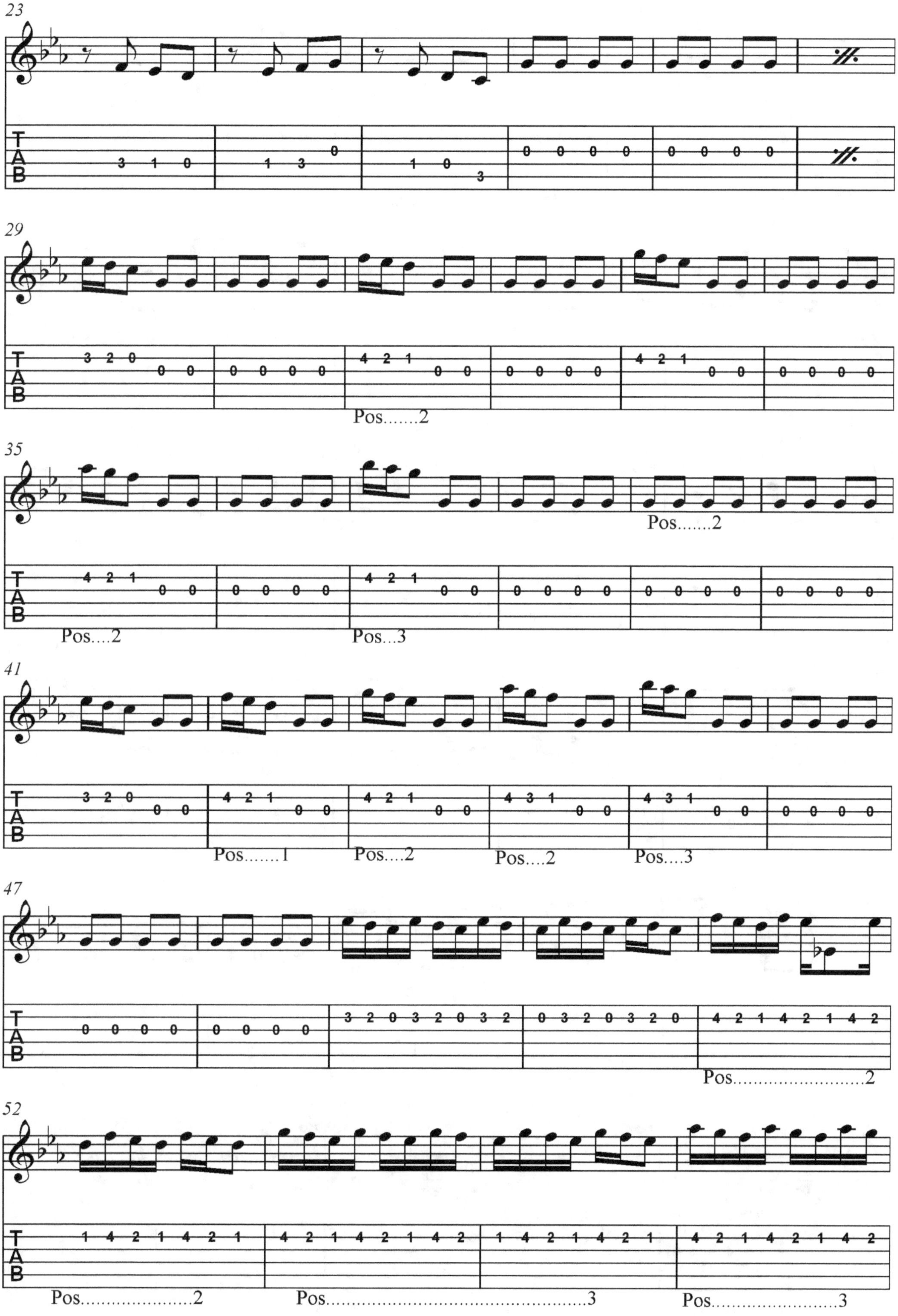

65

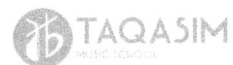

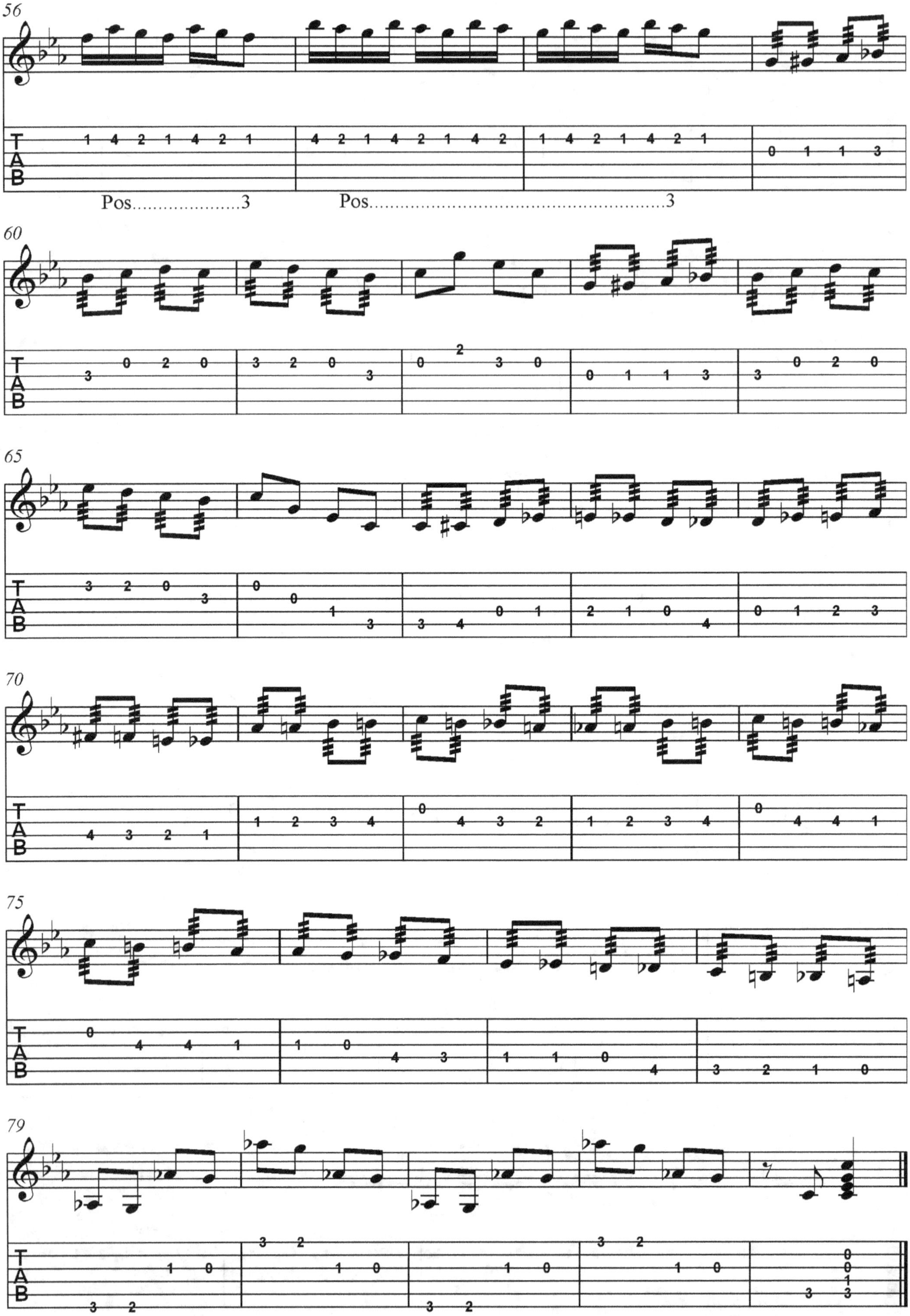

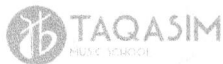

Babylonian Fingers – Ahmed Mukhtar

This piece is one that is written in a way that needs to be played using the thumb and index finger rather than with a *risha*. This way of playing the oud was used about 1,300 years ago (mid-7th century) before the *risha* was introduced. Chords are strummed by using either the thumb or index finger. Usually, the low-pitched notes/*qarar* notes are played using the thumb, while the high-pitched notes/*jawab* notes are played using the index finger.

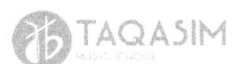

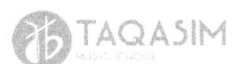

68

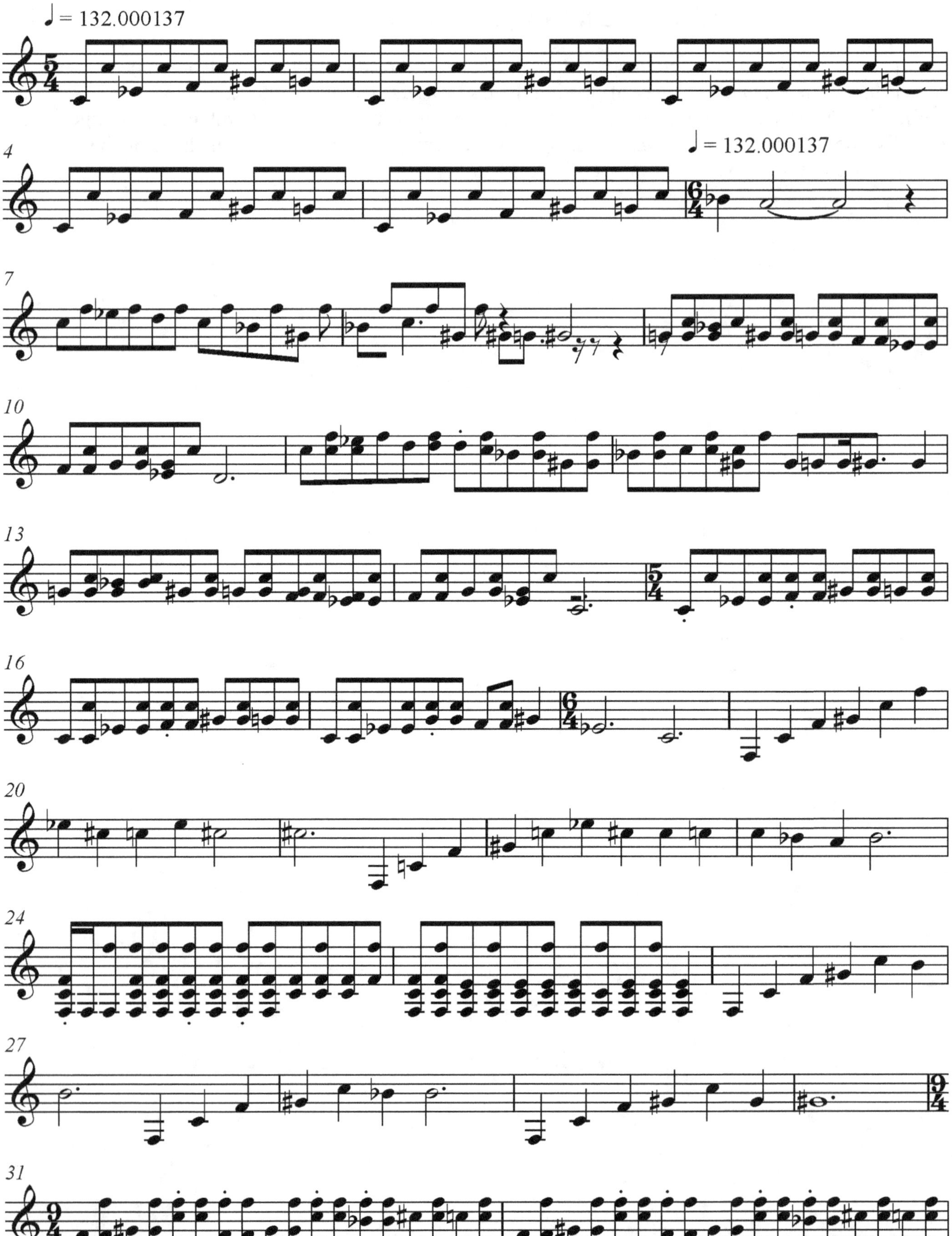

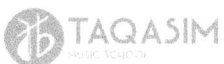

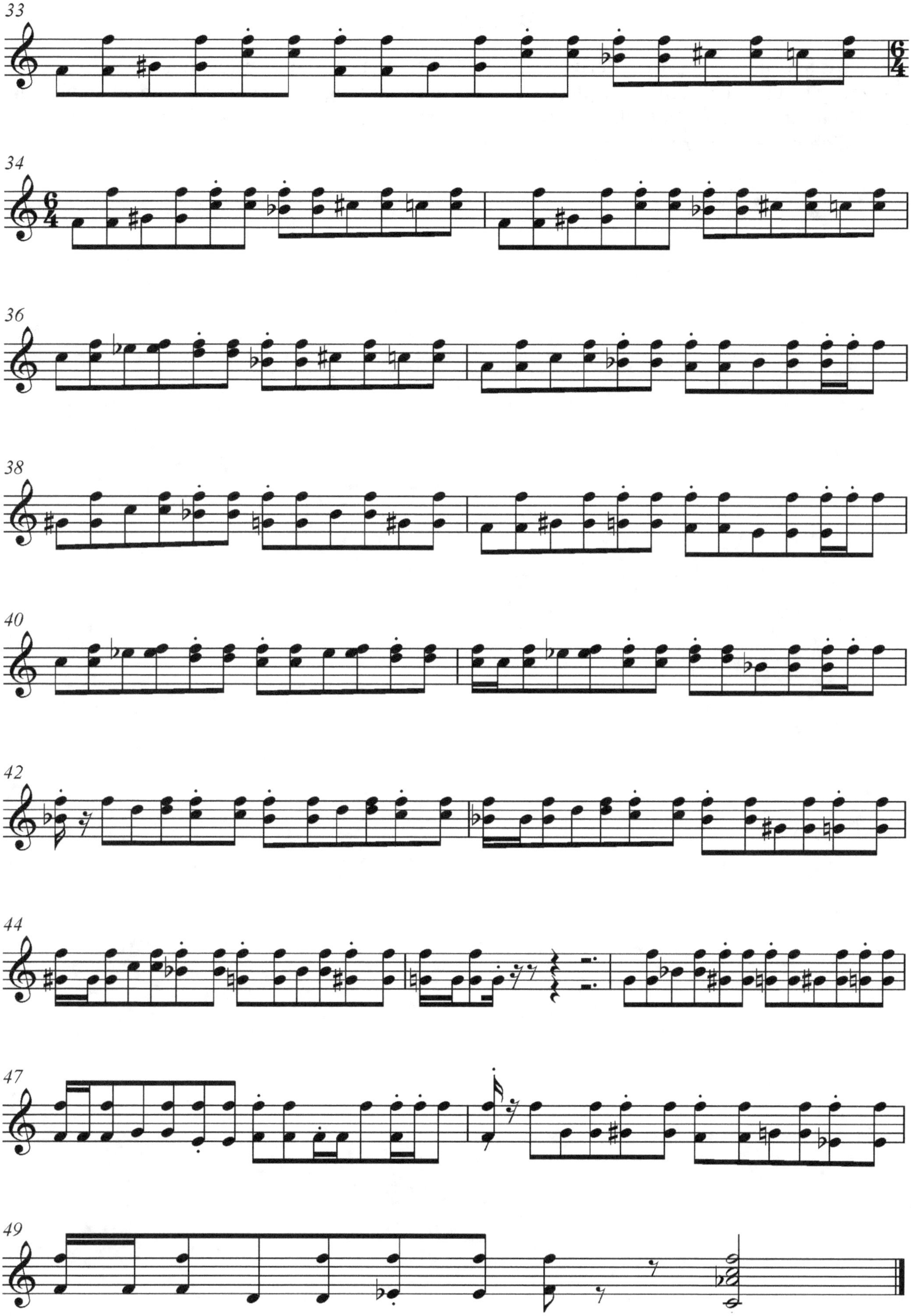

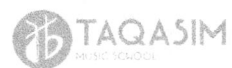

Caprice Form

Caprice is a form of composing derived from an Italian style of composition. It is usually extremely fast and uses a lot of triplets. Its aim is to show a high level of technique when playing a particular instrument. In Arabic music, a Caprice shows both a high level of technique as well as highlights the spirit/*rouhiyyah* of the *maqam* being used.

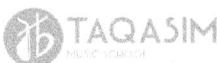

Caprice Nahawand Do – Jamil Bashir

This piece is one that uses a lot of triplets and fast risha movements. Complex syncopation is also used in bars 23 to 26. It uses the first position on all strings and the 2ⁿᵈ and 3ʳᵈ positions on the last string. This kind of playing is called "L-shaped" due to the shape the hand traces on the oud's neck when moving down the 6ᵗʰ string. The piece can be viewed on YouTube.

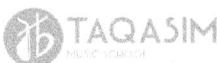

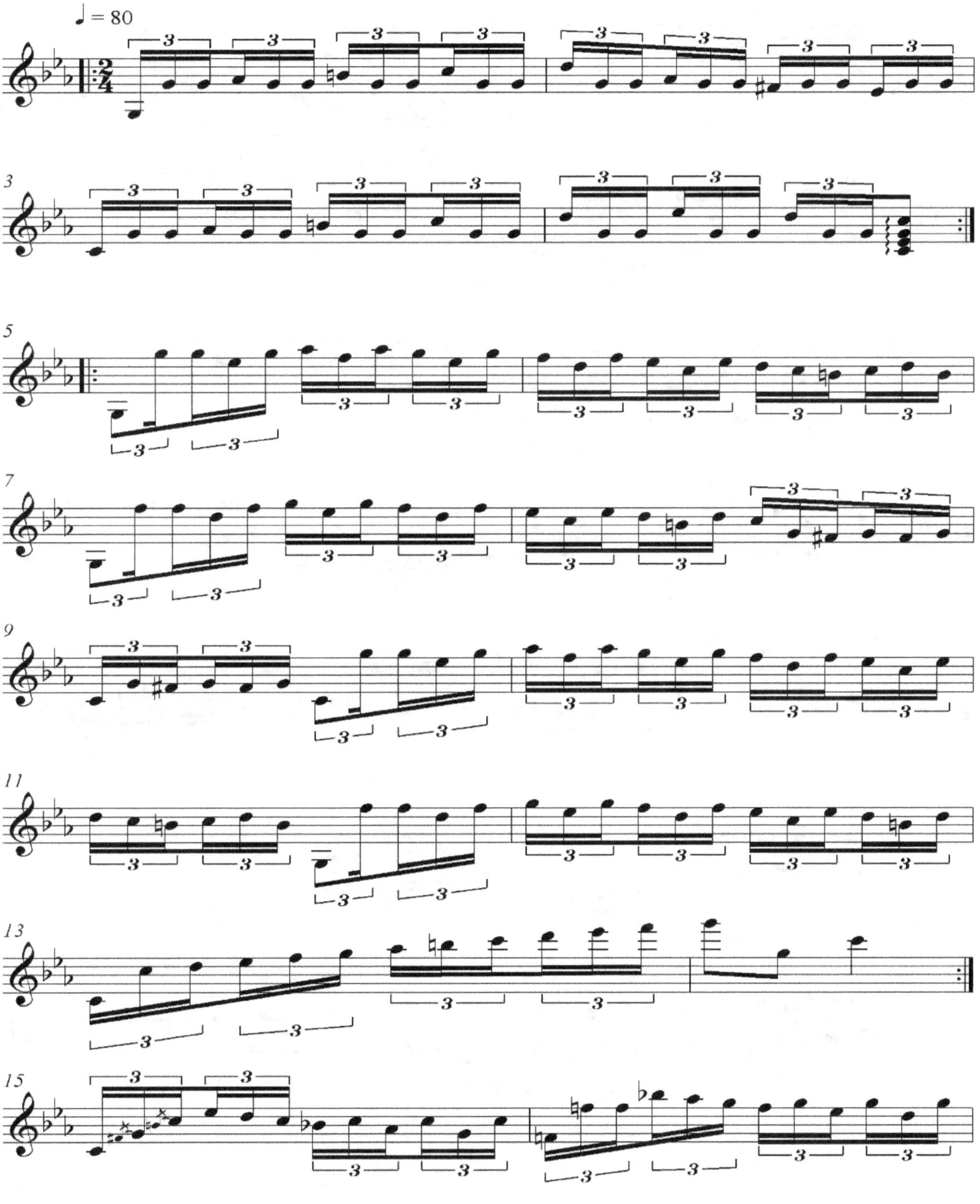

71

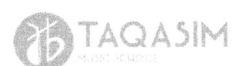

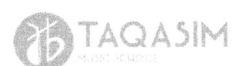

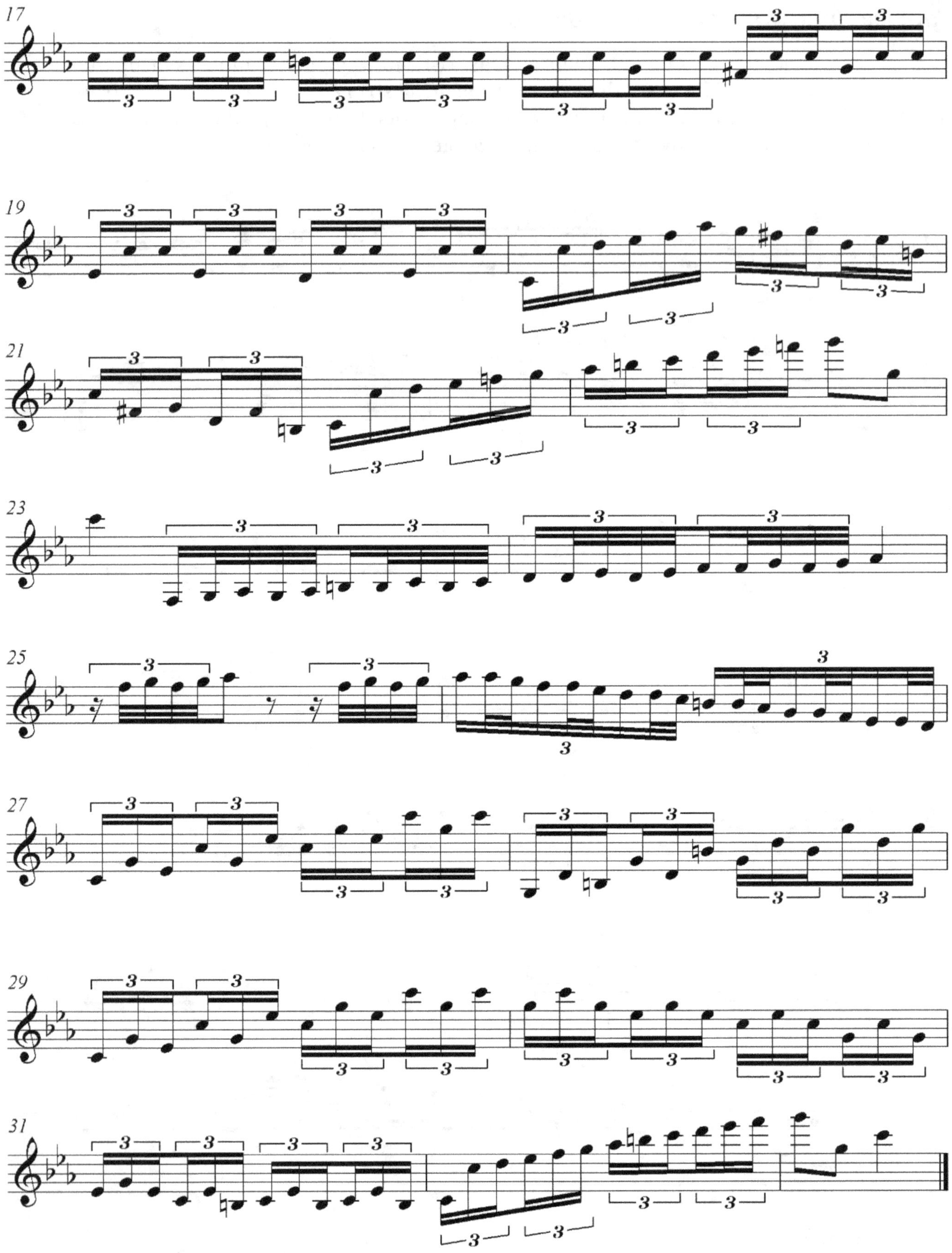

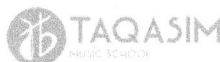

Caprice Nahawand Fa – Jamil Bashir

Here, *Caprice* Bashir has been transposed to Nahawand Fa because different finger positions, octaves and possibilities for ornamentation are used. This provides a good opportunity to practice a different set of skills as well as work on showcasing the *rouhiyyah* of the *maqam* used.

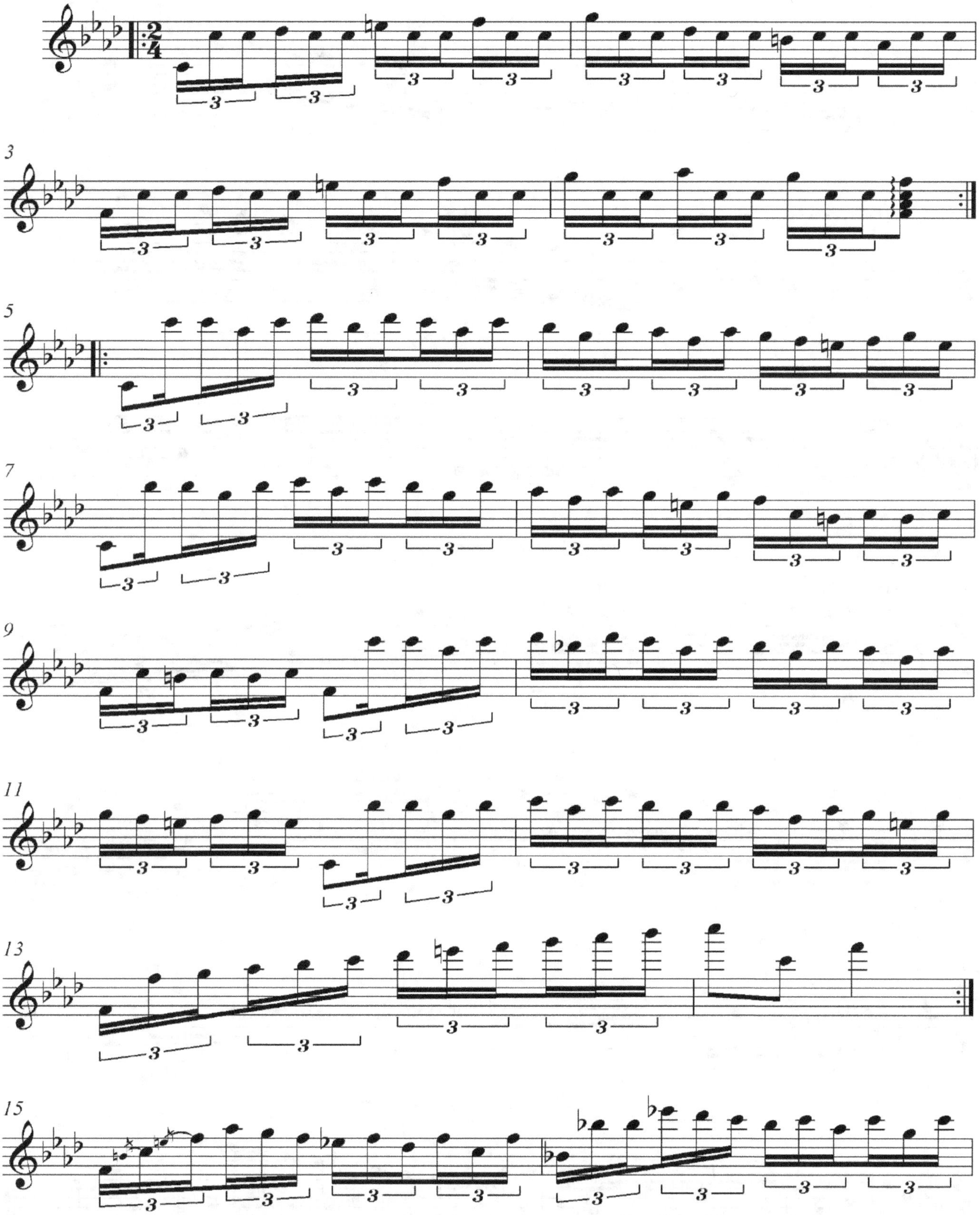

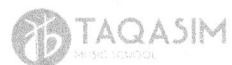

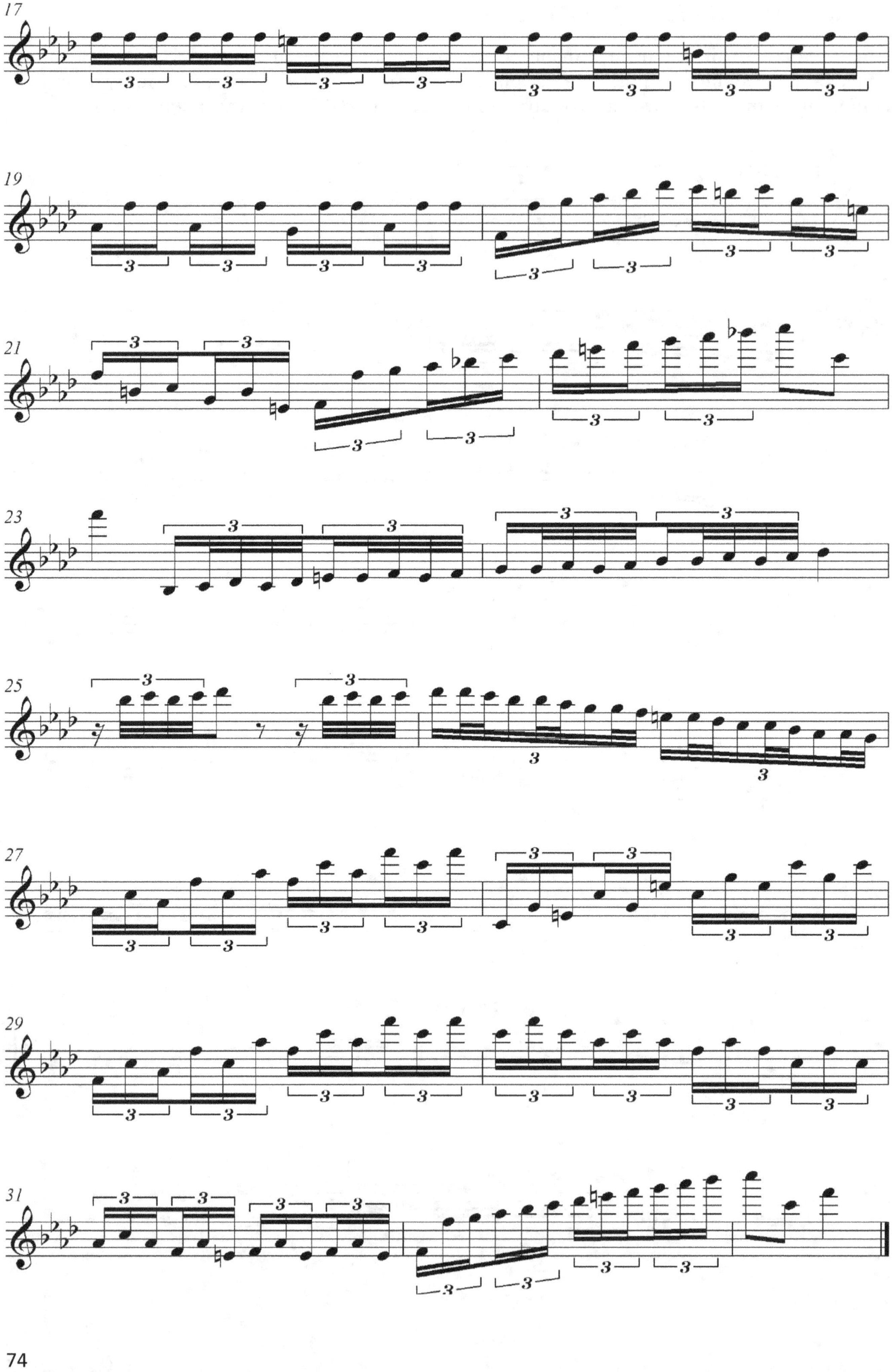

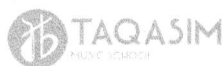

Awtar Ha'ira (*Samaa'i Nahawand* Fa) – Khalid M. Ali

The piece can be viewed on YouTube.

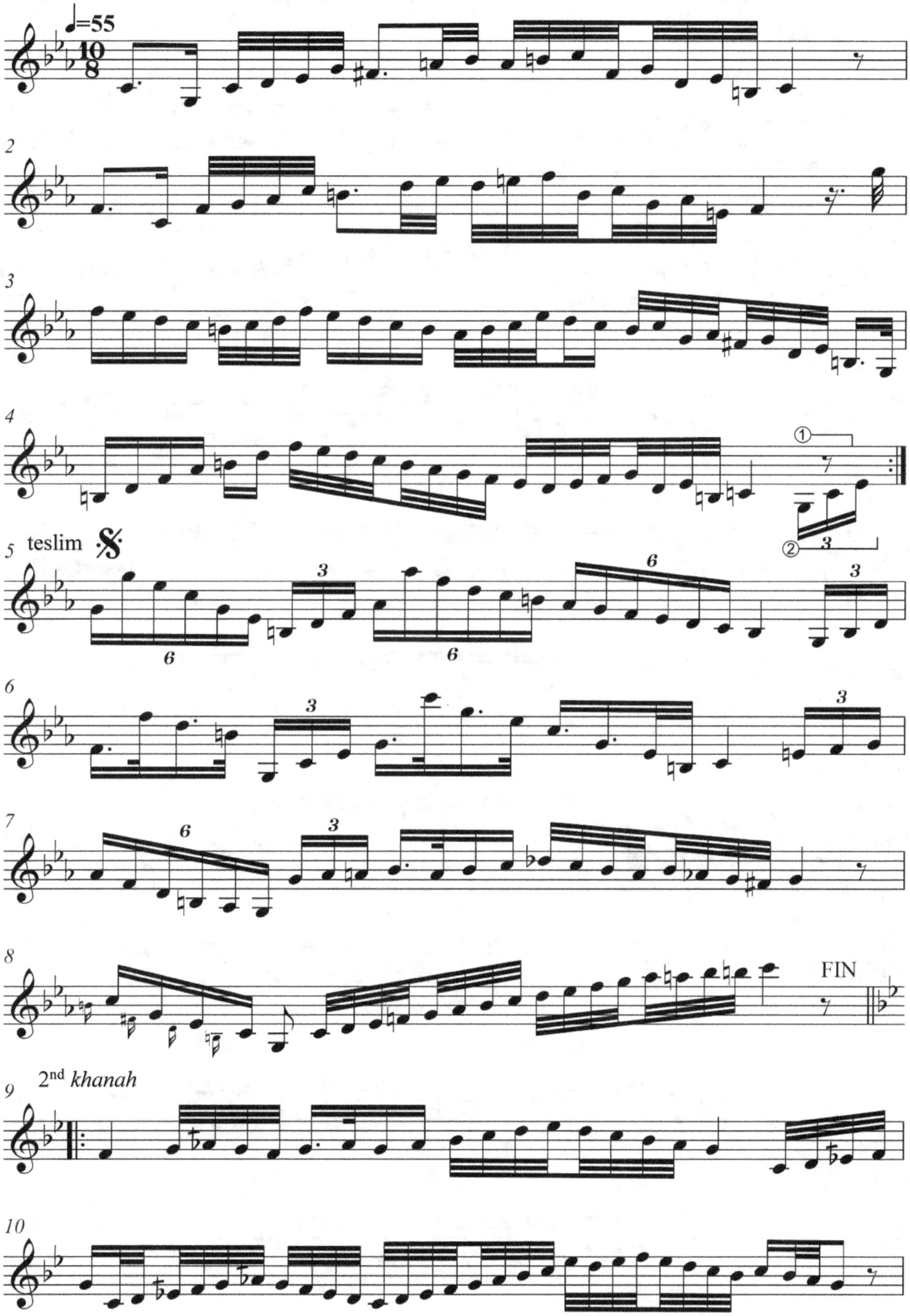

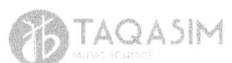

76

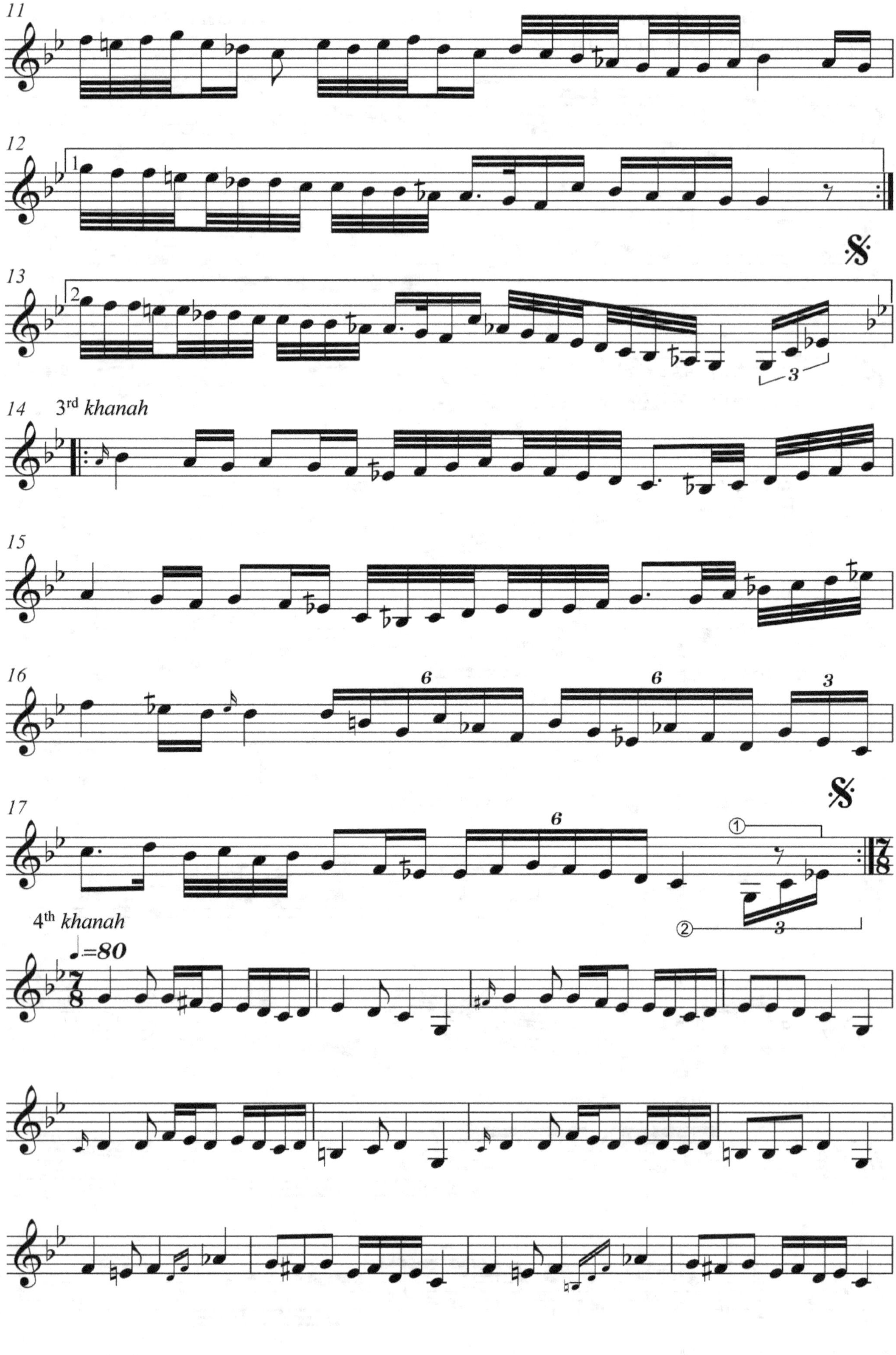

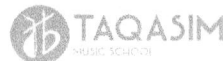

Dance on *Rast* – Ahmed Mukhtar

This piece is extremely sensitive in terms of tonal precision and the use of all three positions combined with the 2nd and 3rd octaves. Many quarter-tones are used in all three positions where distances are narrow. Playing Dance on Rast successfully will depend a lot on the player's ability to listen to precise tonality. Bar 28 combines the use of quarter-tones and arpeggios. The speed at which the piece needs to be played makes it even more difficult. Pay close attention to bars 19 to 27 which uses 3/4 rhythm within the 4/4 tempo.

The piece can be viewed on YouTube.

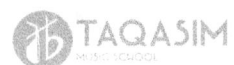

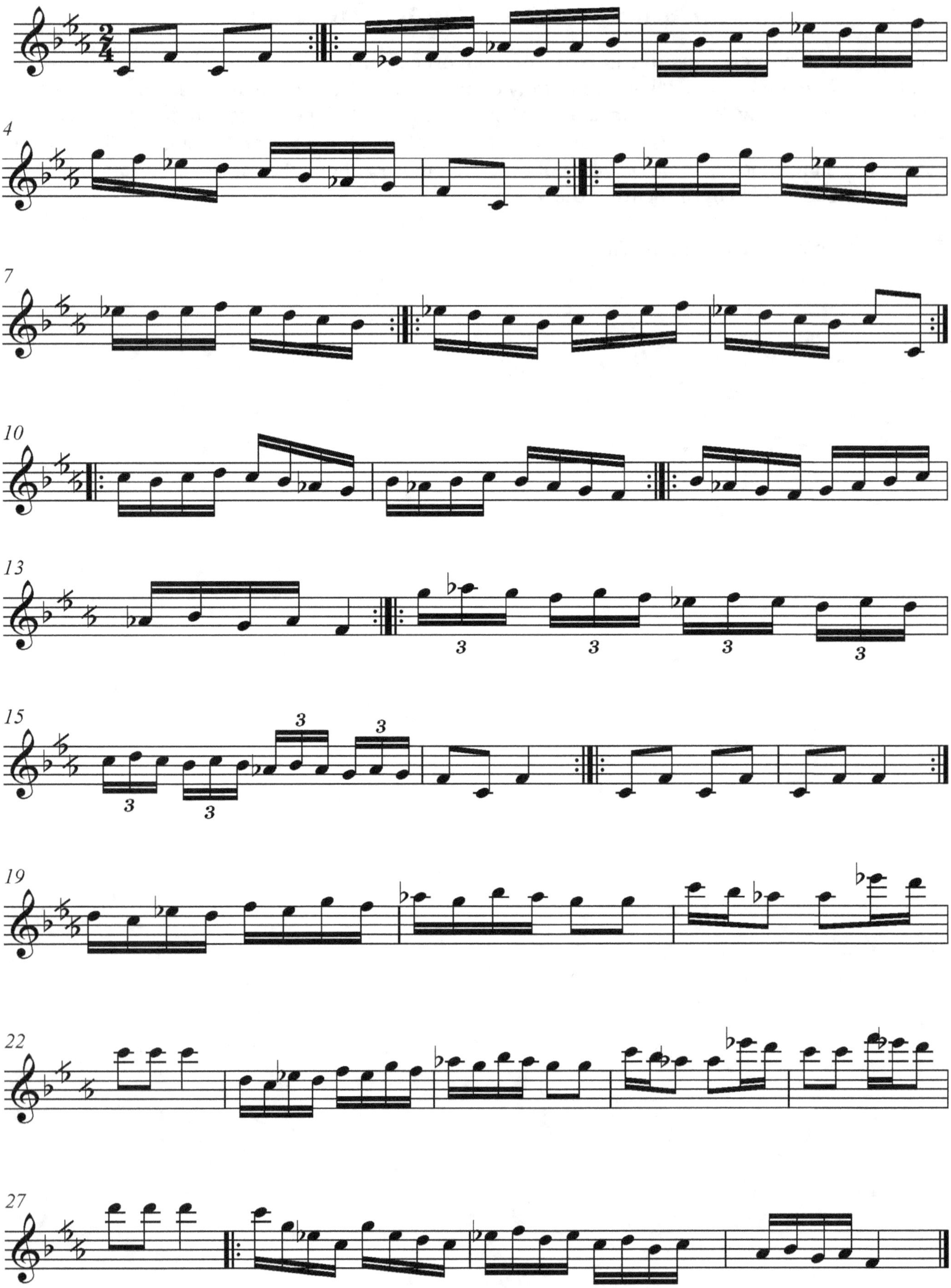

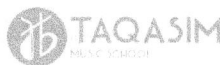

Shurouq (*Rast* Do) – Jamil Bashir

Shurouq, written in *Rast* Do, uses mi half-flat and si half-flat extensively, as both notes are part of the *Rast* Do scale. Once familiar with the piece, complex ornamentation can be applied to highlight the feeling conveyed by the *maqam* itself.

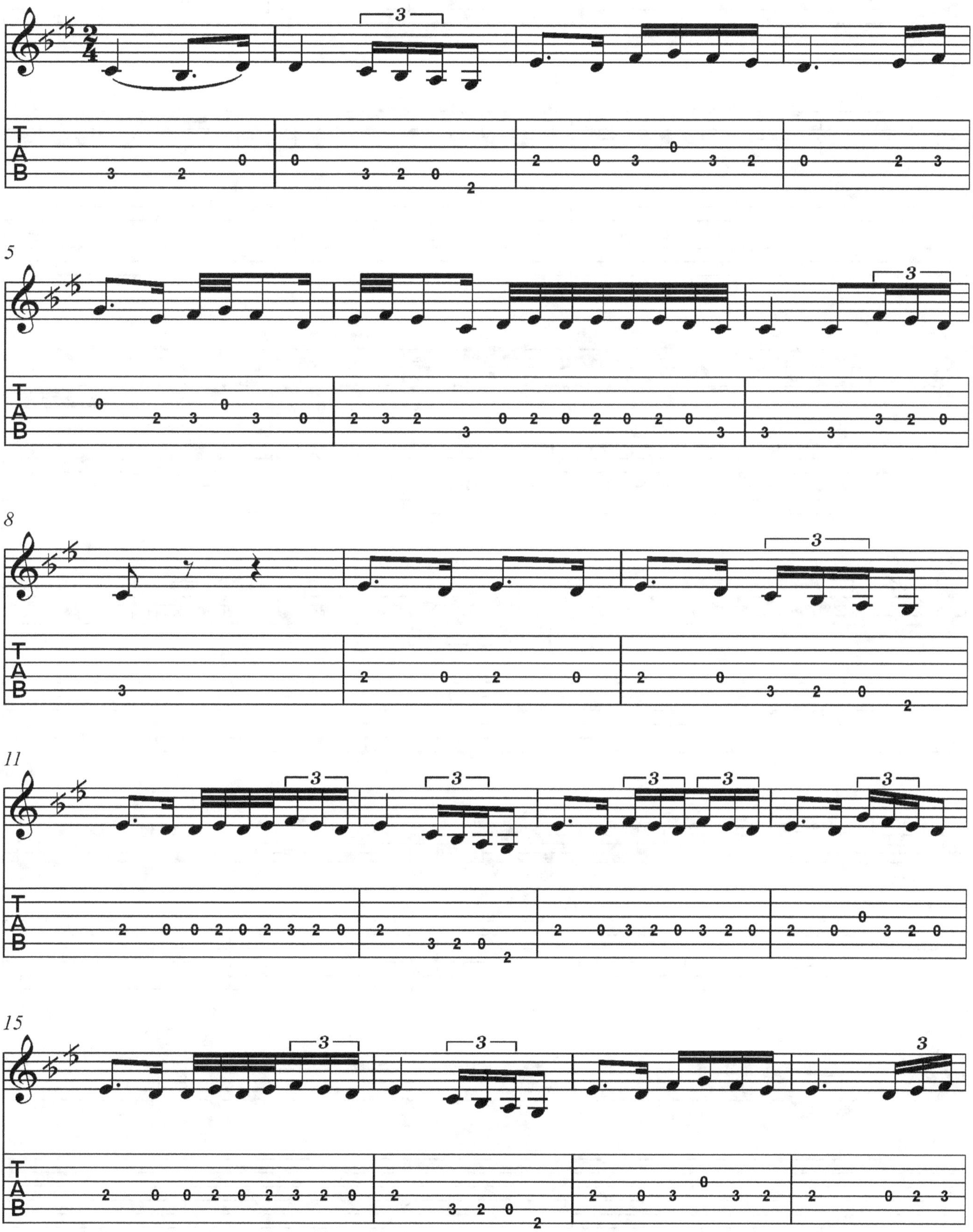

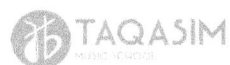

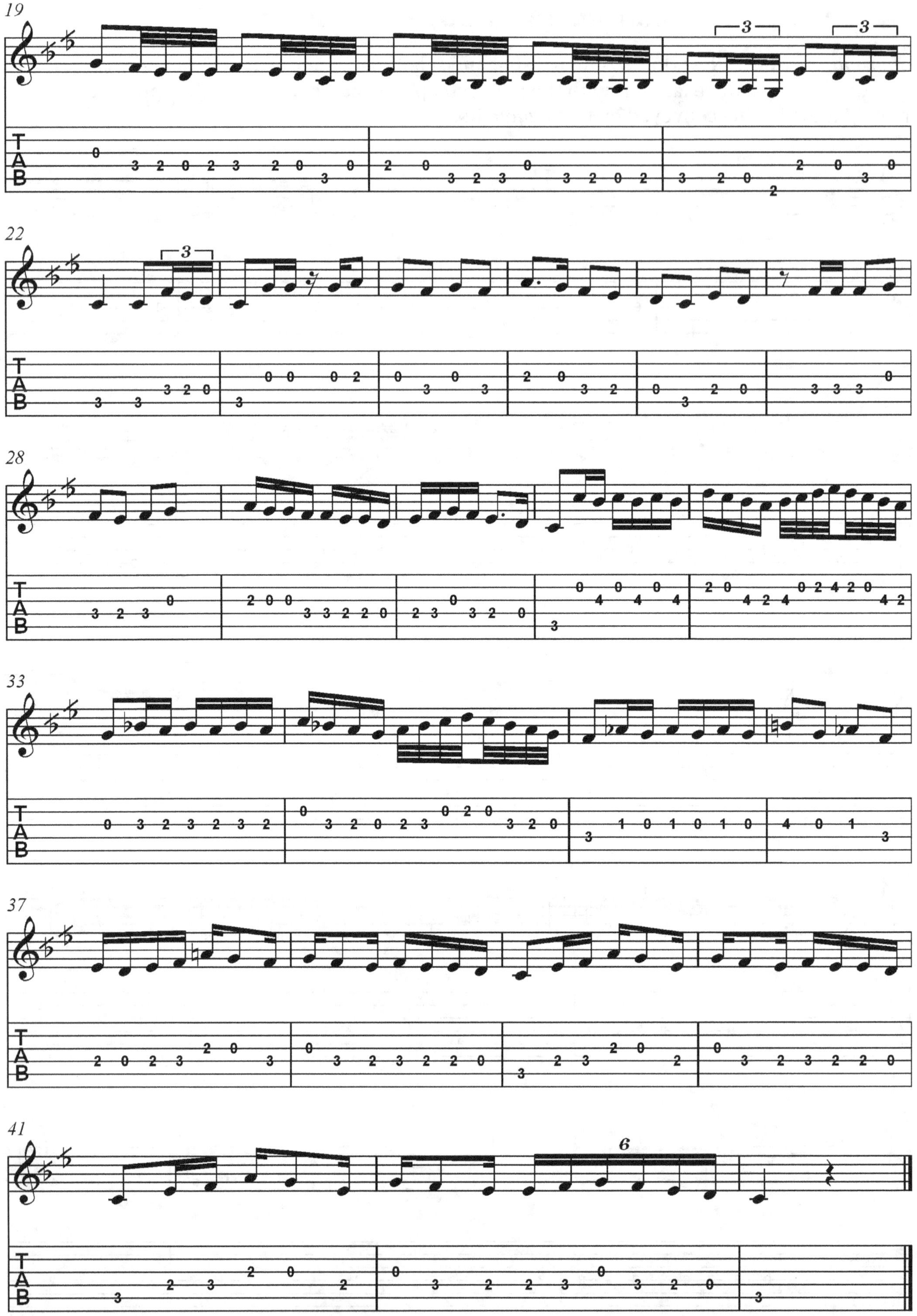

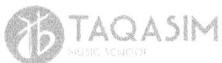

Maqam Shot Araban

Maqam Shot Araban is a secondary maqam from the *Hijaz* family.

Shot Araban Sol

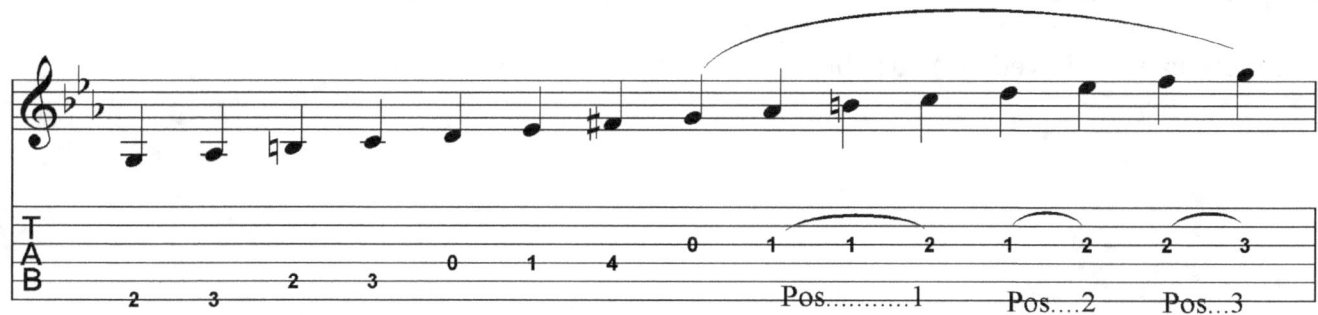

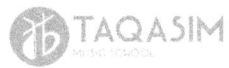

Shahrazad (Darij Samaa'i) – Ahmed Mukhtar

This piece is unique and complex in the way in which it mixes between the *Samaa'i* and *Darij* forms. The first *khanah* is written in *Maqam Shot Araban* using the *Samaa'i* rhythm 10/8. The second *khanah*, written in *Rast* Fa and *Suznak* Fa, switches to using the *Darij* rhythm of 12/10. The third *khanah* is written using *Huzam* Mi in the 1st and 2nd positions in an L-shape playing technique. The fourth and final *khanah* is written in *Kurd* and *Nahawand* Fa, going back to the *Darij* 12/10 rhythm.

The piece can be viewed on YouTube.

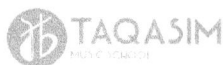

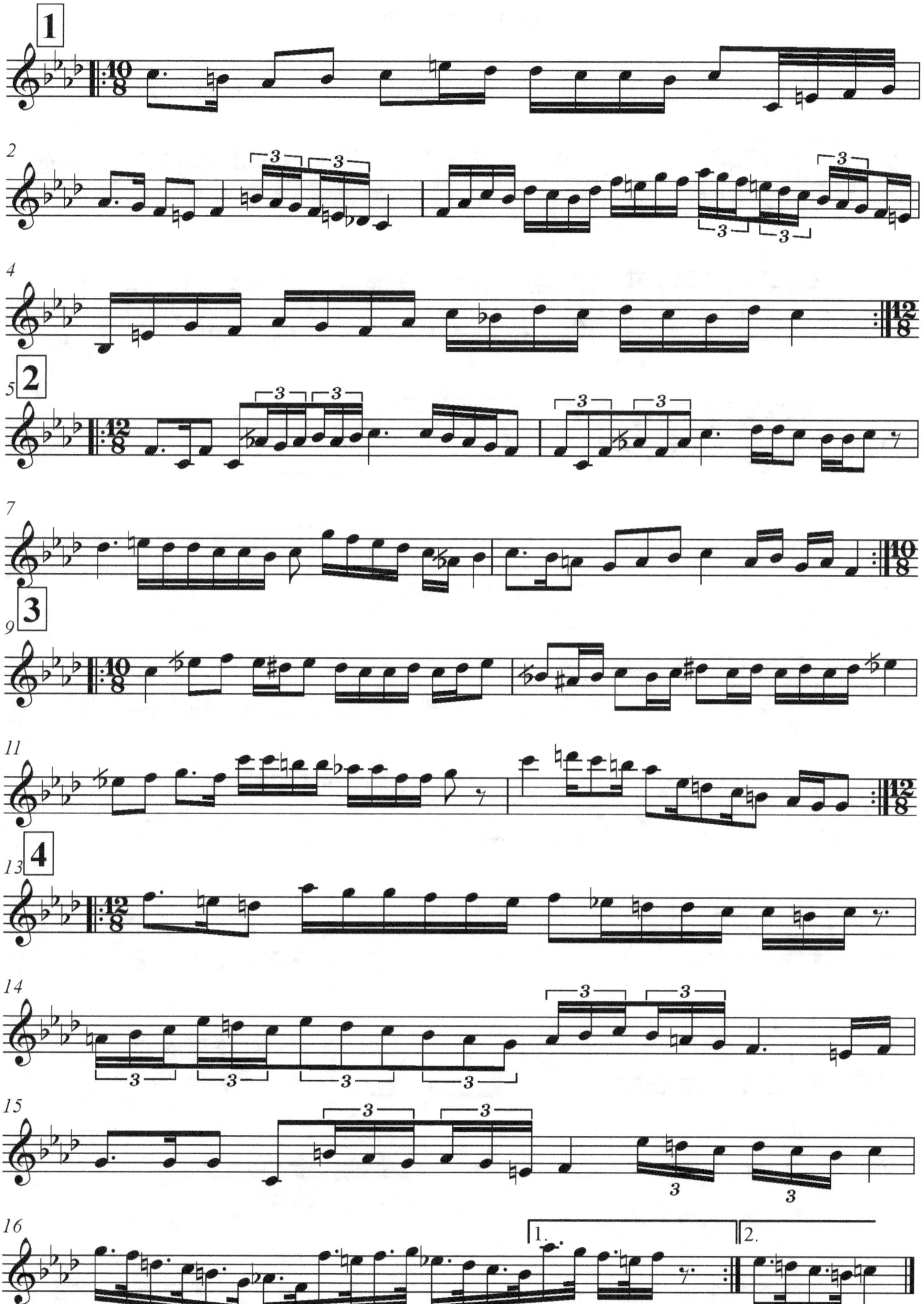

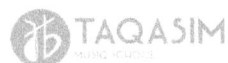

Samaa'i Shot Araban – **Khalid M. Ali**

This piece is one that is useful to practice as it uses full sentences that are written on the *qarar* (bass) notes played on the first and second strings. Double notes are also used.

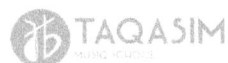

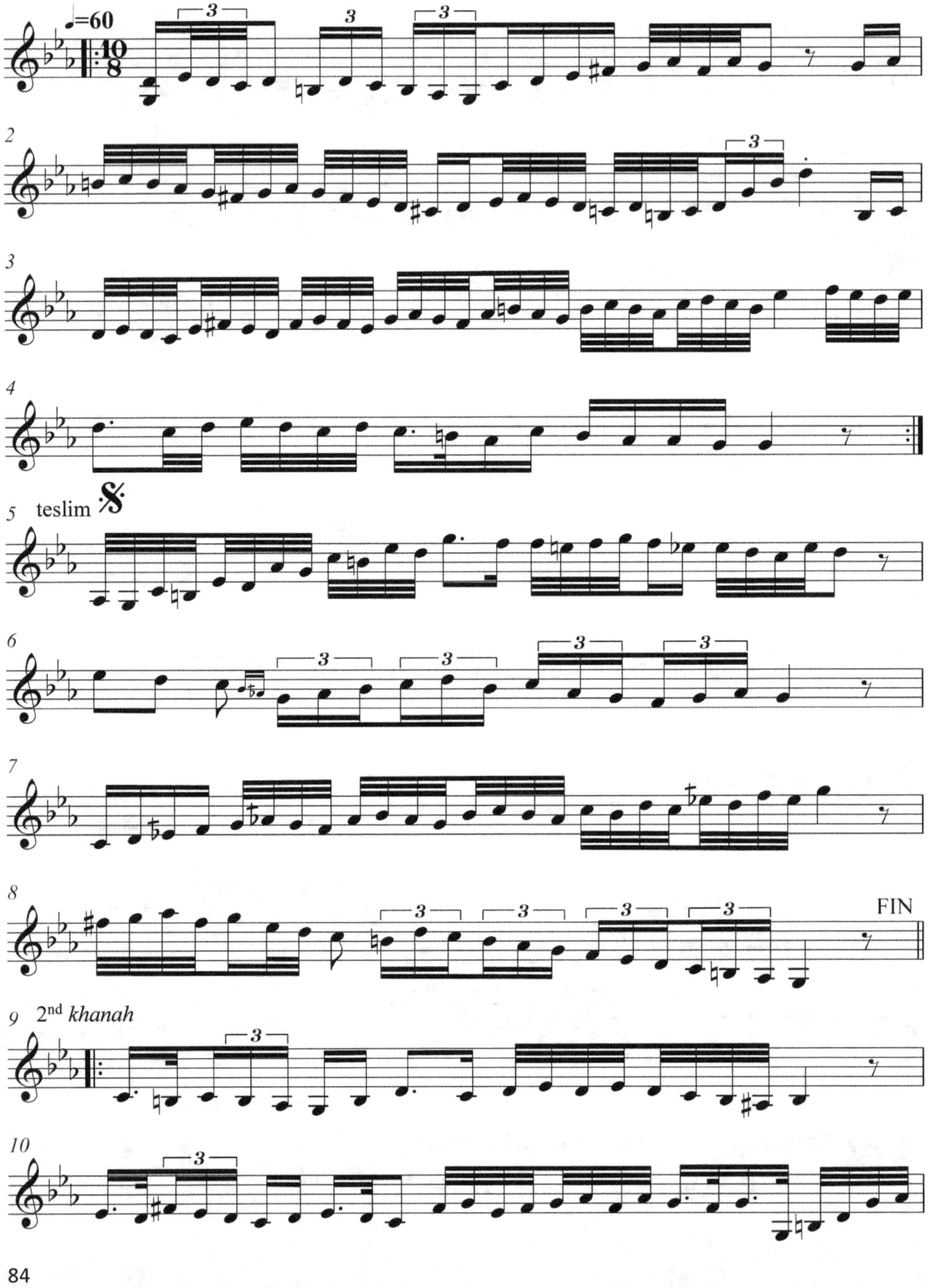

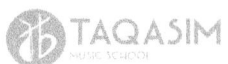

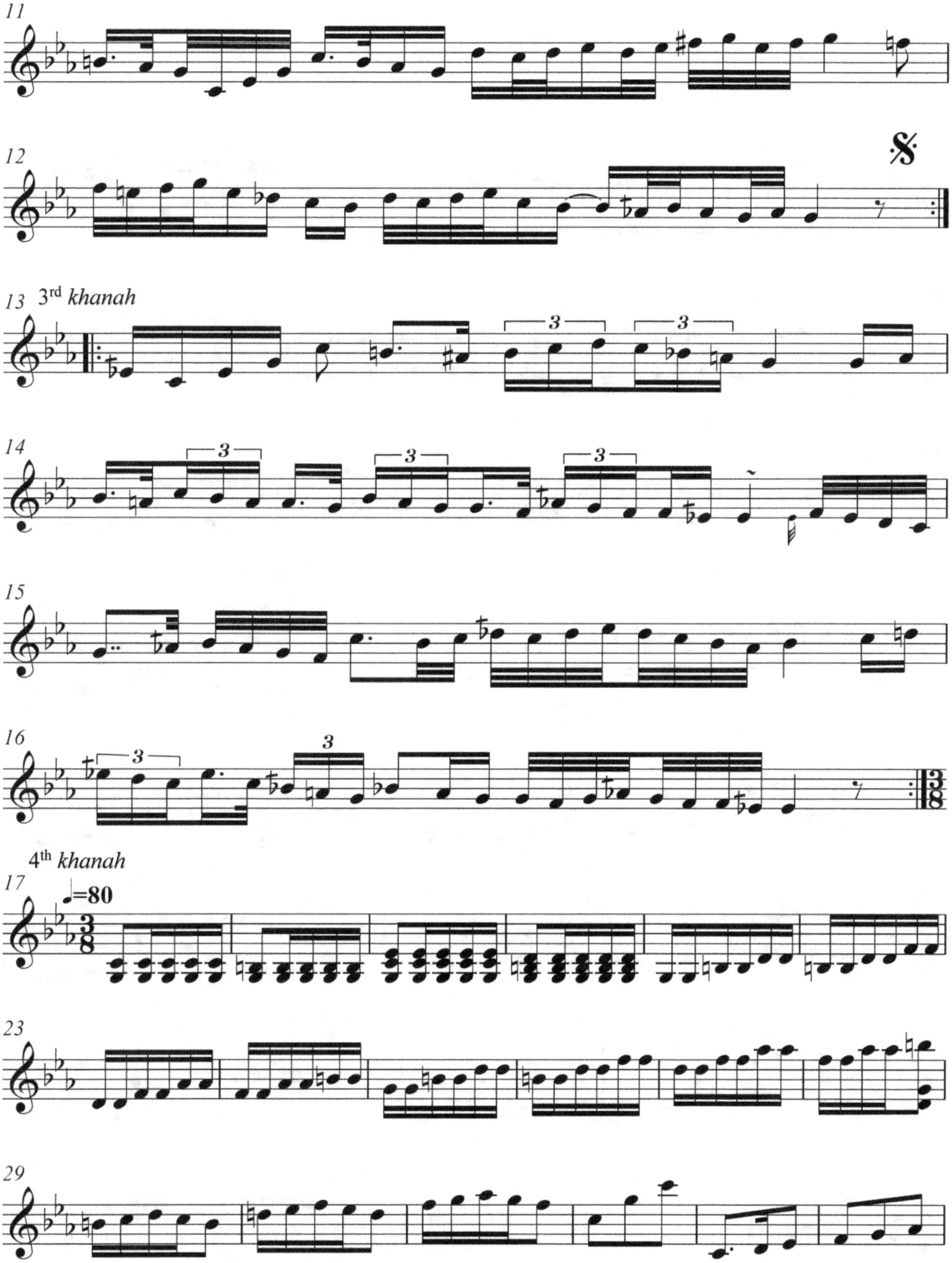

11

12

13 3rd *khanah*

14

15

16

4th *khanah*

17 ♩=80 3/8

23

29

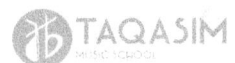

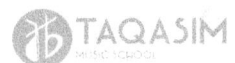

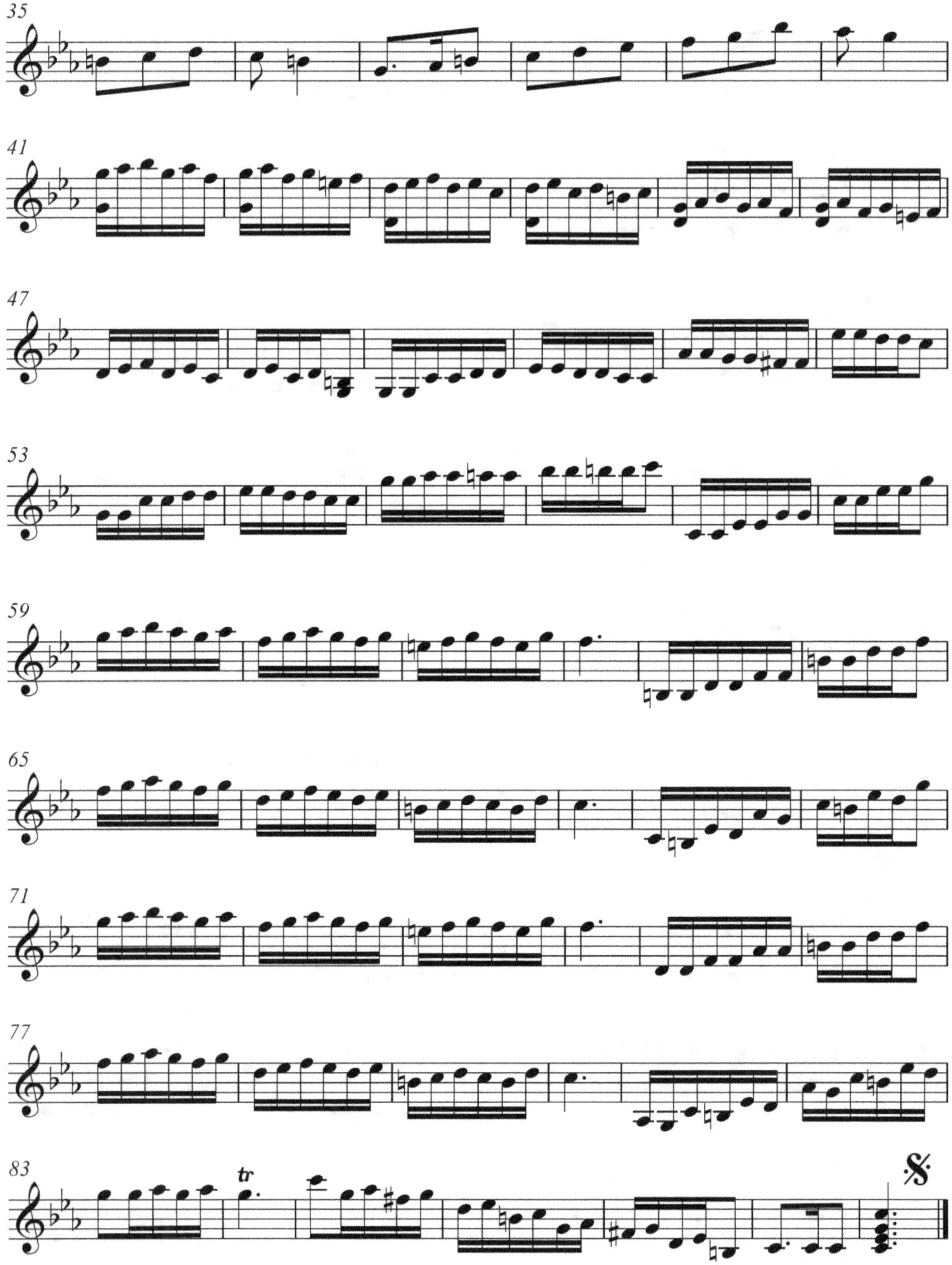

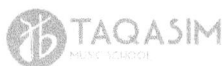

Samaa'i Bayat Sol – Ahmed Mukhtar

In this *samaa'i*, each *khanah* modulates to 2 *maqamaat* rather than just 1 *maqam* as in traditional *samaa'i-s* . The 2nd *khanah* is written in *Bayat* Do and *Hijaz Kar* Do. The 3rd *khanah* is written in *Maqam Nahawand* Sol and *Maqam Lami* La, and the 4th *khanah* uses *Maqam Ajam* Do and *Kurd* Re. The 4th *khanah* contains two part. The first is based on an 11/16 rhythm and the second is written in 3/4.

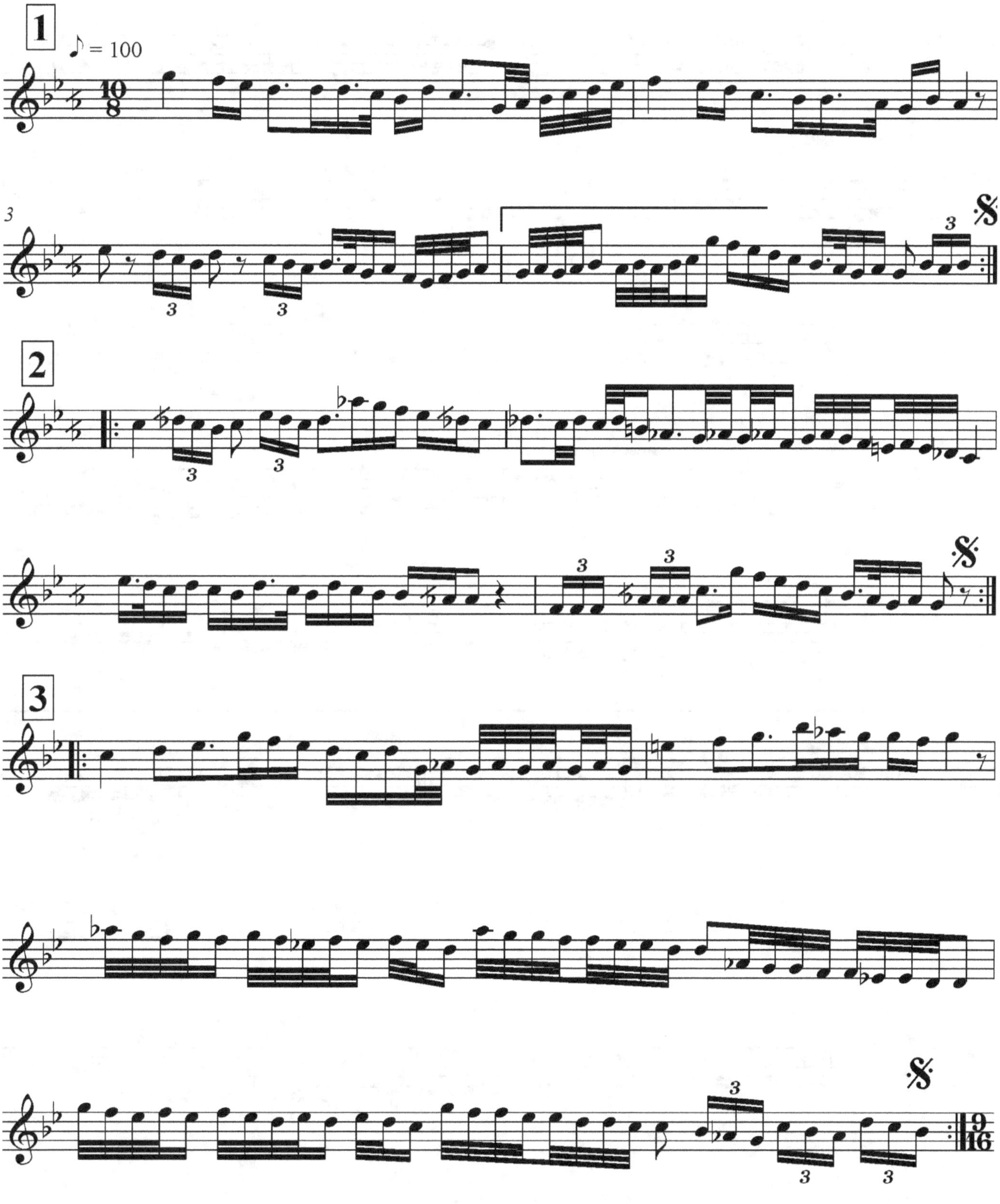

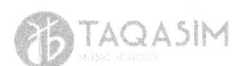

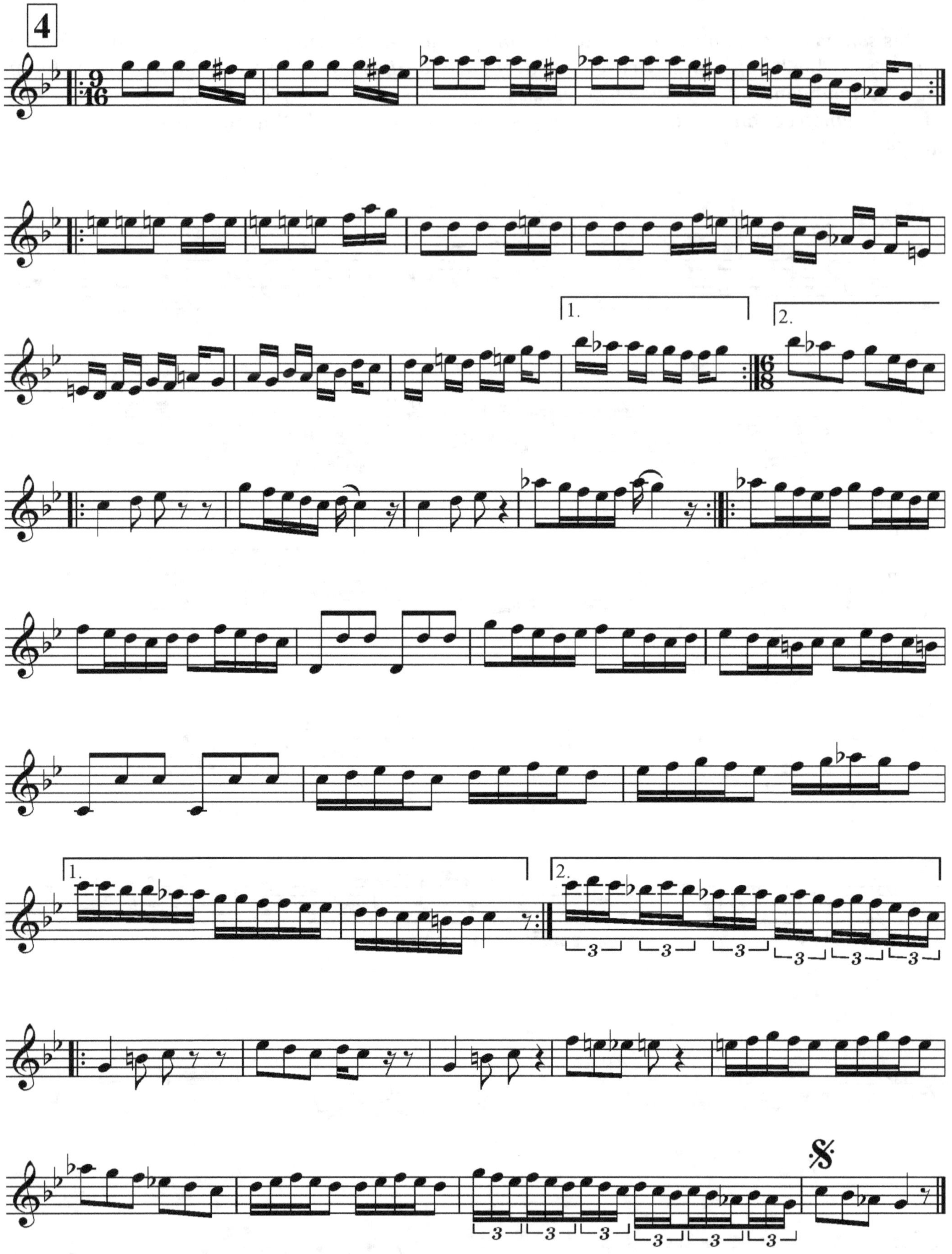

Samaa'i Maqam Rahat al – Arwaah – Khalid M. Ali

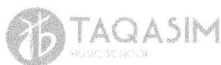

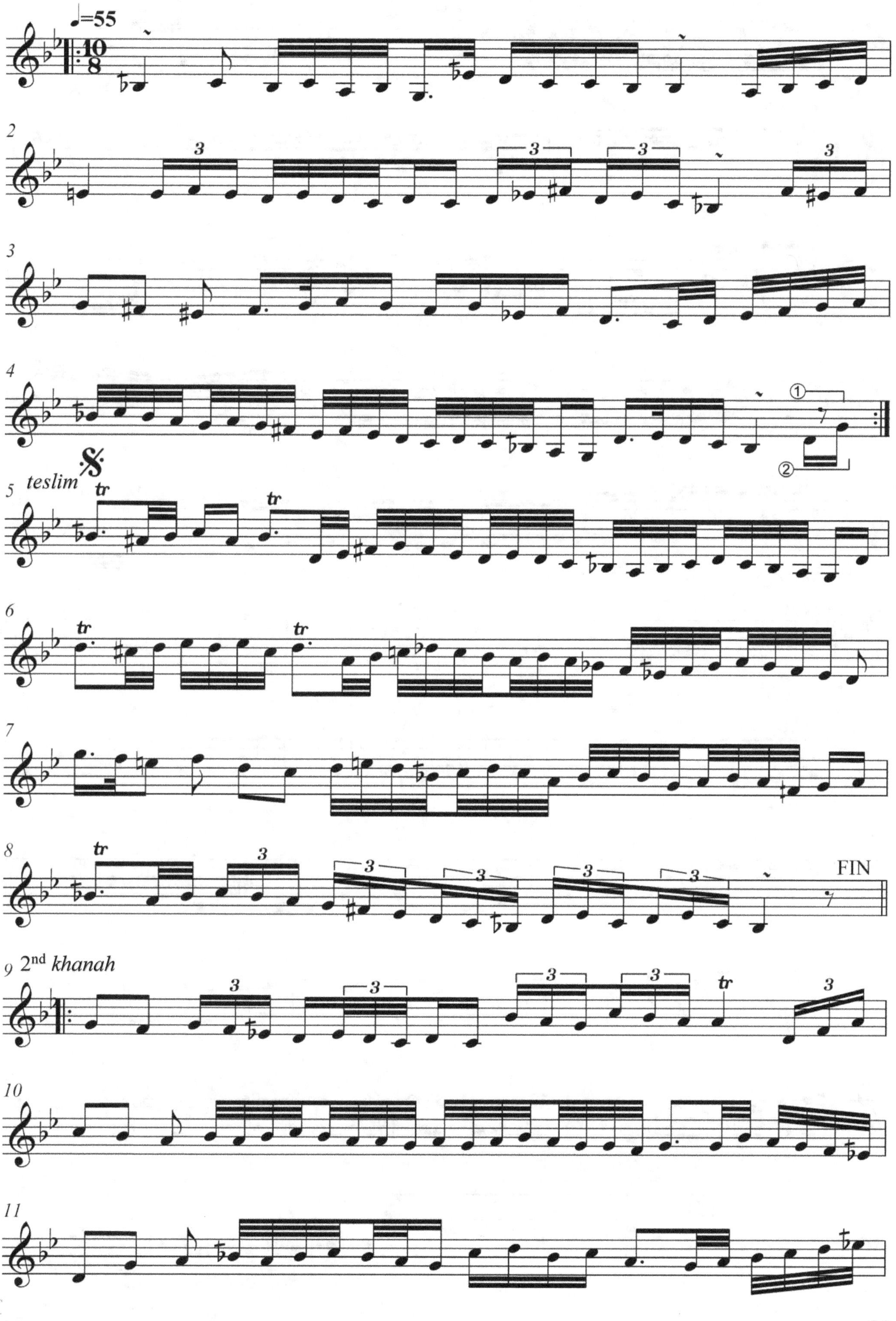

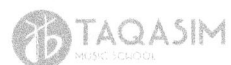

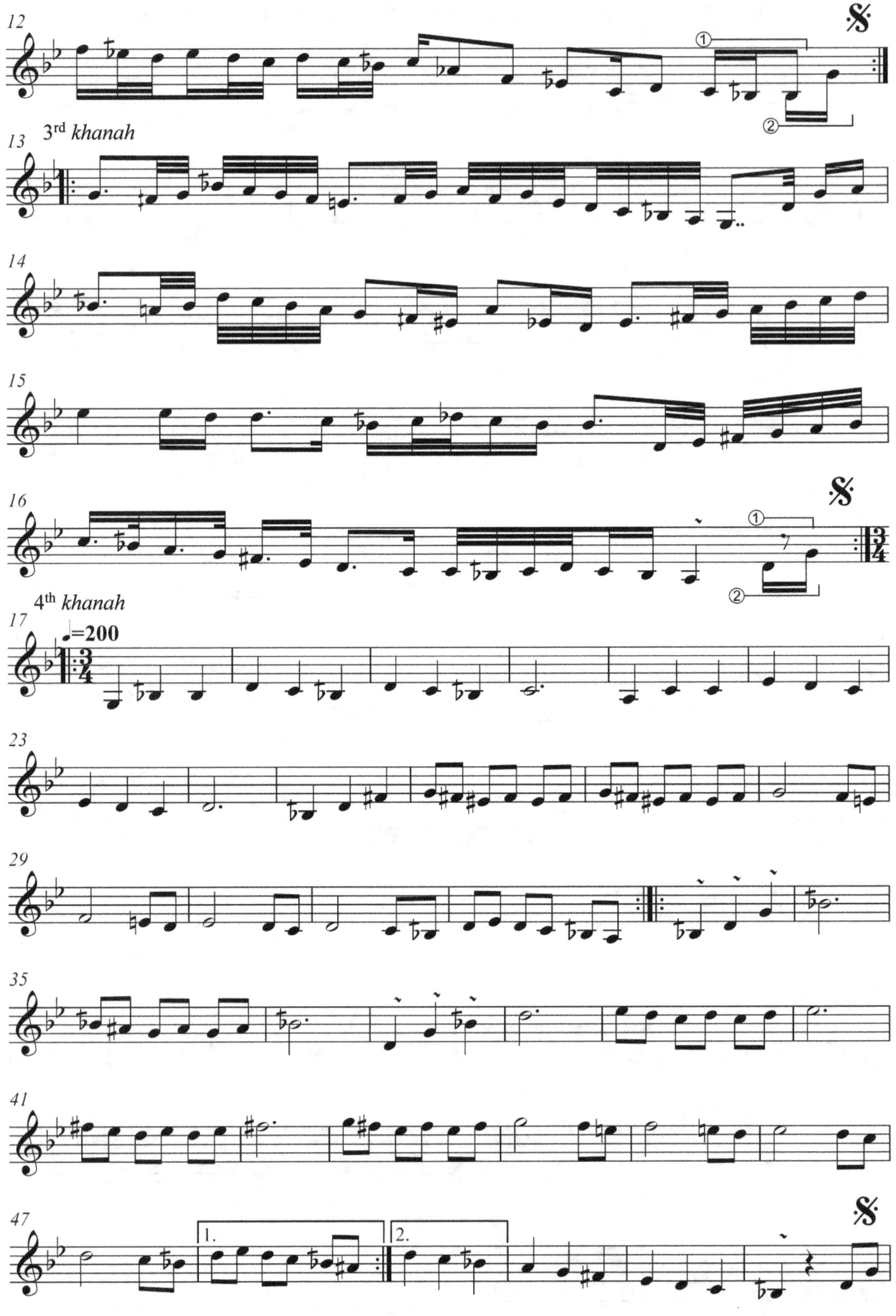

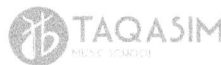

Ahmed Mukhtar

Born in Baghdad, Mukhtar has been playing the oud and Arabic percussions since 1979. In 1983, he began studying both the oud and percussion at the Institute of Fine Arts in Baghdad. A few years later, in 1990 he attended the High Institute of Music in Damascus where he continued his studies of the oud and Western percussions. In 1999, Mukhtar earned an MA from the London College of Music, and in 2003, he received a Masters Degree in Performance with a focus on Middle-Eastern and Arabic music from SOAS (the School of Oriental and African Studies), London.

Timeline

- **2003** MA in Performance – SOAS, London
- **1999** MA from the London College of Music
- **1990** Studied Oud and Western percussion at the High Institute of Music, Damascus
- **1985** Worked extensively with Arabic orchestras and performed on Iraqi TV
- **1983** Studied Oud and Percussion at the Institute of Fine Arts, Baghdad

Roles

- Chairman of the Taqasim Foundation
- Founder and Director of Taqasim Music School
- Member of the High Committee of the Babylon International Arts & Cultural Festival, Hilla, Iraq
- Producer and presenter of the "Solo Program"/"عزف منفرد", Al-Fayha, Iraqi TV
- Former Musical Director – Sleep Song project in France
- Former Director – Iraqi Music Week

Awards

- **2015** Award for Excellence in music composition
- **2009** Alhambra Award for Excellence under auspices of the Queen of Britain
- **2003** Chosen to be 1 of 16 artists to record original work a CD released by the UN benefiting victims of terrorism and war
- **1999** Award for Best Non-Western Musical Composition from the Musicians Union, UK

Discography

- **2015** – Babylonian Fingers
- **2005** – Road to Baghdad
- **2003** – Rhythms of Baghdad
- **1999** – Words from Eden
- **1997** – Tajwal (Live Oud Recital)

Other Work

- Author of the Mukhtar Method series: learn the oud, darbuka & Arabic music theory
- Musical compositions for TV programs including MBC, ART, Al-Mustakela and BBC5
- Theatre: Music composed for "The Soldier's Tale"; an Iraqi/Eurpoean rendition of Stravinsky's classical work directed by Andrew Bigley, performed at The Old Vic Theatre, London, UK in January 2006
- Musical Theatre: Music for "My Name is Jamal". by Algerian Director Abdul Nasser Khalaf
- Poetry: "Baghdad Open Sky" Music composed for the readings of dramatic poetry written by Saleh Al-Hamada
- Film: "Al-Baghdadi" a film by British/Iraqi director Mayham Riada; winner of The Gold Award at the International Filmmaker Festival

www.ingramcontent.com/pod-product-compliance
Lightning Source LLC
Chambersburg PA
CBHW081100180526
45170CB00005B/1830